VOLUME ONE
ISSUE ONE
MARCH 2004

HOME
CULTURES

AIMS AND SCOPES

Home Cultures is an interdisciplinary journal dedicated to the critical understanding of the domestic sphere, its artefacts, spaces and relations, across timeframes and cultures. Whether as a concept or a physical place, "home" is a highly fluid and contested site of human existence that reflects and reifies identities and values. The Journal aims to promote a conversation about the domestic sphere across the many disciplines in which "home" forms a key unit of analysis. By generating a site for interdisciplinary discussion and comparative approaches, *Home Cultures* provides a vital and diverse forum for our general understanding of this vital sphere of human activity.

Towards this aim, the editors invite submissions from a broad range of scholars and practitioners, including: design practices, design history, social history, literary studies, architecture, gender studies, cultural/social history, anthropology, sociology, archaeology, urban planning, legal studies, contemporary art, geography, psychology, folklore, cultural studies, literary studies and art history.

Anyone wishing to submit an article, interview, book, film or exhibition review for possible publication in this journal should contact the editors,

Victor Buchli
v.buchli@ucl.ac.uk
University College London

Alison Clarke
alison.clarke@uni-ak.ac.at
University of Applied Arts,
Vienna

Dell Upton
du2n@cms.mail.virginia.edu
University of Virginia

Or write to
homecultures@ucl.ac.uk

Notes for contributors can be found at the back of the journal.

ISSN: 1740-6315

SUBSCRIPTION INFORMATION

Three issues per volume.
One volume per annum.
2004: Volume 1

ONLINE
www.bergpublishers.com

BY MAIL
Berg Publishers
C/o Customer Services
Extenza-Turpin
Blackhorse Road
Letchworth
Hertfordshire SG6 1HN
UK

BY FAX
+44 (0)1462 483011

BY TELEPHONE
+44 (0)1462 672555

INQUIRIES

Editorial: Kathryn Earle, Managing Editor, email: kearle@berg1.demon.co.uk

Production: Ken Bruce, email: kbruce@bergpublishers.com

Advertising and subscriptions: Jenny Howell, email: jhowell@bergpublishers.com

SUBSCRIPTION RATES

Institutions' subscription rate £125/US$195

Individuals' subscription rate £45/US$72*

*This price is available only to personal subscribers and must be prepaid by personal cheque or credit card

Free online subscription for print subscribers

Full colour images available online

Access your electronic subscription through www.ingenta.com or www.ingentaselect.com

REPRINTS FOR MAILING

Copies of individual articles may be obtained from the publishers at the appropriate fees.
Write to

Berg Publishers
1st Floor, Angel Court
81 St Clements Street
Oxford OX4 1AW
UK

Printed in the UK by Henry Ling Ltd, Dorchester

Daniel Miller, University College London, UK

Gerald Pocius, Memorial University, Canada

Martin Raymond, Viewpoint, UK

Suzanne Reimer, University of Southampton, UK

Elizabeth Shove, University of Lancaster, UK

Ilya Utekhin, European University at St Petersburg, Russia

US EXHIBITION REVIEWS

Shelley Nickles, Smithsonian National Museum of American History, USA

UK BOOK & EXHIBITION REVIEWS

Clare Melhuish, University College London, UK

HOME CULTURES
VOLUME 1
ISSUE 1
MARCH 2004

CONTENTS

HOME CULTURES   VOLUME 1, ISSUE 1.   REPRINTS AVAILABLE   PHOTOCOPYING   © BERG 2004
PP 1–4   DIRECTLY FROM THE   PERMITTED BY LICENSE   PRINTED IN THE UK
               PUBLISHERS.   ONLY

EDITORIAL

VICTOR BUCHLI
ALISON CLARKE
DELL UPTON

The launch of *Home Cultures* represents the beginning of long-over-due discussion about the domestic sphere across many disciplines. Curiously, until now, there has not been a specific 'home' for the study of this area. The Editors have each felt somewhat cut off from other disciplines, as disciplinary boundaries and traditions have isolated scholars who take the domestic sphere as their primary unit of analysis. Consequently, it has often been rather difficult to find out what others in various fields have discovered. Discussions seem to be confined within anthropology, architectural history, design history, literary criticism and geography, to name just a few areas where the domestic as a unit of analysis has proven to be particularly pertinent. Yet, this site of analysis is vital in understanding some of the key issues pertaining to the human condition. There we are able to understand diverse and essential aspects of human existence from the self, gender, the nature of individuality, family and social relations, to the wider spheres of architectural space, public and private boundaries, labor distinctions, the nature of the city and the elemental terms of social life in general.

More significantly, the very act of delineating a domestic sphere, at the expense of others, is of course a historically specific exercise that sees this arena as something that grows in complexity, articulation and refraction. Claiming it or delineating it in whatever shape or form is, of course, a deliberate con-stitutional act, tied to historical and contingent particularities of time and place. The autonomy of this realm of human life is often identified as a Victorian phenomenon—a consequence of the social tensions produced by industrial-ization and the segregation of human activity into separate spheres of work and home. As Walter Benjamin once remarked: "The 19th century like no other century, was addicted to dwelling. It conceived the residence as a receptacle for the person, and it encased him with all his appurtenances so deeply in the dwellings interior that one might be reminded of the inside of a compass case, where the instrument with all its accessories lies embedded in deep, usually violet folds of velvet" (Benjamin 1999: 220). While the "home" in the form described by Benjamin may be distinctly nineteenth century, the *household* and the *family* are surely much more broadly distributed notions, however variously they may be defined. So, perhaps one of the challenges we are taking on is the endeavor to understand the variety of relationships between those social insti-tutions and their material site or manifestation.

Of course, in early years and in other societies and times, the boundedness of the home is not so readily discernible and, like the notion of the liberal autonomous self, with whom the home is bound up ("embedded in the deep, usually violet folds of velvet") in indigenous Western traditions, it is delineated in different fashion, constitutive of different selves or not constitutive at all. The domestic sphere has been the focus of social reform from the *Utopia* of Thomas More, the Encyclopedists of the eighteenth-century, to nineteenth-century so-cialist reformers such as Charles Fourier, John Ruskin, and their twentieth-century heirs. Socialist revolutionaries, Feminists, Modernist architects and designers at work on the ideal human habitation invoked the image of the primeval hut of the first man Adam (Rkywert 1989), in the worker's house, and the essential moral terms of existence as developed within the "existenz minimum."

The home is the site where the ego is forged, moral subjects produced, represented, enacted, pathologized, witnessed and judged. At the opening of the twenty-first century, the home is increasingly fragmented and refracted as the pluralities of lifestyle, self and space are refashioned and new technologies forge new forms of individuation with their attendant social relations, reconfigured families, households and communities. As Cullens (1999) has said, the con-temporary home is in many ways the last realm of the utopian—where every-one is now free to realize their selves, and their lifestyle, as part of this attenuated and atomized utopian practice—and the focus for the major part of our consumer economies and collective wealth as individuals. Yet, the home, increasingly one of the central nodes of information space and the consumer economy of the World Wide Web, is subject to the incursions of surveillance, radio waves, mi-crowaves, mobile phone transmissions, etc., that deny its Victorian sanctity. The home is increasingly the live/work dwelling that is also the "last place that 'the utopia of a renewal of perception' is allowed to go" (Cullens 1999: 221) when it has failed so spectacularly in broader realms of social life since the collapse of communism.

But, as the corporeal self in all its diverse forms is universally and intuitively intelligible so too is the space that the self dwells "embedded" within. For this reason, we are as much concerned with Paleolithic dwellings as we are concerned with the homelessness of the twenty-first century. Needless to say, this tradition, as the notion of the unified skin-bound self, and those other modern categories we once felt comfortable with, such as gender, sexuality and others, are highly problematic in terms of the ways these categories are produced within the domestic sphere under conditions of increasing flux and fragmentation.

How these boundaries are negotiated has never been more troubling theoretically and methodologically, as they affect so many realms of inquiry that no one discipline can achieve a sense of what has been and is at stake. This first issue of the Journal expresses the unstable and problematic nature of these boundaries and what they are forging. As can be seen from the many diverse approaches from different fields of inquiry, it is only through such collective, interdisciplinary projects that this complexity can be grasped and communicated—as we hope to achieve through this first collection of articles and in others to come in future issues of this Journal.

Of course, the problem of boundaries is where we delineate the so-called domestic apart from the public, and whether we can segregate these two at all, calls into question categories of public and private, self and social. These are controversial distinctions and elisions, which have never been straightforward at any time or in any place. It is for this reason that a journal such as *Home Cultures* cannot be, in the strict sense, devoted to some intuitive and highly subjective category of the home but rather towards its problematic and fluid nature. Therefore, we will strive to include as great a breadth of essays as possible—be they textual or visual—which address this problematic topic. We welcome scholarly articles across disciplines, as well as contributions from practitioners (designers and artists) working in this area. The preoccupation with the domestic sphere has not been restricted to conventional scholarly disciplines, rather it has been the subject of thorough and critical investigations in design and the visual arts. The dialog between these various fields has been flitting and tantalizing, but there is greater scope for closer investigation and collaboration as, so often, the visual arts employ the methods of the social sciences and vice versa—retracing an effort that goes back to the birth of the Western empirical tradition itself. It is hoped that we can enhance the resonances between these fields through submissions to this Journal.

Politically, the domestic sphere forms the touchstone of some of the bitterest of current political and social battles faced by nation states and their communities. However, the domestic sphere is probably one of the least appreciated yet single most important arenas of political action—having been the focus of utopian and revolutionary concern since Thomas More's day—as well as of a reactionary political nostalgias and repressive social imaginaries. One might also say that the domestic sphere or the home is the lived political and social space in which the social facts about ourselves are forged, tested and made true; as such, it is also necessarily dystopian, and pathological. It is also one of the least understood and most methodologically challenging areas of human life, necessarily cut off from other spheres of interaction—who can really know what goes on behind closed doors? Additionally, the home is the single most important investment of financial resources any individual makes, be it in a traditional society or under late-capitalism.

As ubiquitous and as straightforward as it may seem, the domestic sphere is also very elusive. It is in this field that often the most subaltern forms of identity can be studied, that their necessarily ephemeral traces of existence be understood, from the micro-morphological analysis of household spaces in archeology to those fleeting ephemeral activities of little consequence that make up most of our daily lives and experiences, and within which the primary terms of existence of the voiceless, inarticulate and abject are often revealed. The dwelling is often seen metaphorically as a shell or exoskeleton supporting human life and, as such, it shares similarities with geological metaphors of time and evolution through tantalizing legibility of these physical traces. (Consider here Rachel Whiteread's "House" as death mask or the dissections of Gordon Matta-Clark.) Study of the dwelling complements studies of the body: that "corpus delicti" whose traces and clues are left within the home. Here, Marx's fossil metaphor still prevails as the fossil is what remains of the "indwelt" surface of living beings: those "Relics of bygone instruments of labour possess the same importance for the investigation of extinct economic forms of society, as do fossil bones for the determination of extinct species of animals" (Marx 1986: 78).

Interest in the domestic and dwelling as such has been a political artefact from its very beginnings and the foundation of all modern discussions of social and political life. Unquestionably such a project as the one put forth here is itself political in light of the ever-more fraught and problematic character of the domestic sphere. However, the goal of this Journal is not partisan, or transformative—change and political work will continue with or without the intervention of journals such as this. Instead, it is hoped that issues raised here within the scholarly space that the Journal creates will help us make sense as individuals and collectively as scholars with the increasingly intractable and stressful nature of the domestic sphere in which each and everyone of us is embedded in one way or another.

REFERENCES

Benjamin, Walter (1999), *The Arcades Project*. Cambridge, MA: Belknap Press of Harvard University.

Cullens, C. (1999) "Gimme Shelter: At Home with the Millennium," *Differences* 11(2): 204–27.

Marx, K. (1986), *Karl Marx: A Reader*, J. Elstner (ed.). Cambridge: Cambridge University Press.

Rykwert, J. (1989), *On Adam's House in Paradise: The Idea of the Primitive Hut in Architectural History*. Cambridge, MA: MIT Press.

HOME CULTURES   VOLUME 1, ISSUE 1.   REPRINTS AVAILABLE DIRECTLY FROM THE PUBLISHERS.   PHOTOCOPYING PERMITTED BY LICENSE ONLY   © BERG 2004 PRINTED IN THE UK

PP 5–22

D. J. B. YOUNG

THE MATERIAL VALUE OF COLOR: THE ESTATE AGENT'S TALE

D. J. B. YOUNG TRAINED AS AN ARCHITECT AND WORKED IN THE BUILDING INDUSTRY FOR A DECADE BEFORE STUDYING ANTHROPOLOGY. CURRENTLY A RESEARCH FELLOW IN THE DEPARTMENT OF ANTHROPOLOGY, UNIVERSITY COLLEGE LONDON, HER INTERESTS INCLUDE ANTHROPOLOGY OF ARCHITECTURE. FORTHCOMING PUBLICATIONS CONCERN THE MATERIAL COLOR PRACTICES OF CENTRAL AUSTRALIAN PITJANTJATJARA PEOPLE. PREVIOUS PUBLICATIONS IN THIS AREA INCLUDE "THE LIFE AND DEATH OF CARS" IN *CAR CULTURES* EDITED BY DANIEL MILLER AND A BOOK, *ART ON A STRING*, WITH LOUISE HAMBY, ACCOMPANYING AN EXHIBITION THEY CURATED, WHICH TOURED AUSTRALIA IN 2001–2003.

This article is based on research of estate agents' advice to residential vendors and landlords in inner London. The article discusses the point when the potential value of the property is geared up for realization. In this process the value is assessed by the agent as lying in the "presentation" of the property. This is paradoxical in that the materiality of the dwelling where much of its agency lies, is idealized as "neutral." Color devalues, or at least impedes the velocity of property exchanges. This article seeks to dissect the historiography of "neutrality," the erasures and dematerialization it represents, and its effect on property as commodity and as fetish.

The world of colour is opposed to the world of value.

Baudrillard 1996 [1986]: 31

It is important that potential buyers can visualise themselves in your home—make sure that you keep the decoration clean and neutral and hide the family clutter.

The National Association of Estate Agents

The UK is popularly characterized as a culture obsessed with home ownership and with the housing market. This article concerns London estate agents'[1] advice to their clients and the agent's experience of what sells quickly and what does not. Although location, both the area and more the intimate locale, are the main factors in the market value, the materiality of the building itself also has agency and this article sets out to explore the specific connections between materiality, value, and people.

Anyone perusing the selection of photographs on estate agents websites or in their shop window, might be struck by the uniformity of interiors shown. Pale walls, the occasional yellow—but muted—and wooden floors are ubiquitous. This uniformity increases the more central the location and where there is a predominance of "apartments." It is not a phenomenon confined to the UK. "Neutral décor" is a phrase that currently advertises property for sale and rent in Australia and the USA as well. I will return to the material effect, agency, and historical construction of neutrality later.

In many anthropological studies of housing emphasis is placed on economic structures governing "cultural" ones, for example, Zukin's (1982) influential work on the loft apartment as originating in artistic capital. Studies on the social construction of domestic space and the materializing of social relations have reclaimed agency for the householder against external powers, such as the state, exploring the home as a site of identity, and interior decoration as a process, directed aspirationally at potential others (e.g. Attfield 1999; Clarke 2001). Miller's (1990) study of residents' "appropriation" of an alienating environment on a London council estate examined kitchen fittings and decoration as an objectification of social relationships. These studies have sought to unravel the home as a place of consumption where mobile objects variously offer resistance, memorialization, and escape to the householder (Miller 2001a). Buildings, although static in terms of site, possess a mobility that becomes evident in the circulation of their image, a vital aspect of their marketing. Buildings also possess agency, not only as a personification, objectified in a household ghost, but in their very fabric, a fabric which, as will become clear, is not as solid as it may first appear (Miller 2001b).

In this, the agent's tale, the materiality of the home is, I will argue, made into the look of the immaterial, evoking Marx's "least understood joke—the fetishism of the commodity inscribes immateriality as the defining feature of capitalism" (Stallybrass 1998: 184). As Stallybrass so appositely reveals, for Marx, the materiality of an object was not problematic, but the object as commodity, although it has a form, is only determined by its exchange value; "it's physical existence is 'phantom-like' . . . To fetishise the commodity is to fetishise the invisible" (Stallybrass 1998: 184). The fetish was born through the contact of Europeans with West Africans out of the former's attempts to stabilize the boundary between things and persons, a boundary which, alarmingly, Africans did not have. And yet an object can waver and cross the border between fetish and commodity—it can be both (Spyer 1998). Household things and clothes were where wealth resided for the working class in London of the 1860s, and these could be converted to cash at the pawnshop (Stallybrass ibid). The twenty-first-century Londoner, if she has managed to buy, may accumulate wealth through the object of her home, borrow against it or convert it into cash. London house prices at the end of 2002 were, at over £241,000, nearly *twice* the national average and *five* times the average income of first-time buyers.[2] Yet, as the British media constantly highlight, there has been potential in recent years to earn more than a year's salary in the value increase of a home.

In 2002 over 60% of London housing was owner-occupied and more than 10% rented from a private landlord.[3] In 1961 only 36% of households in London were owner-occupied and 43% were privately rented (Conway 1984). These statistics contain a contested and politically charged arena (cf. Hall and Jacques 1989). A case study of inner London is then a particularly pertinent one in which to examine the relationship between materiality, agency, and the commodification of housing. The research was carried out as semi-structured interviews asking twenty-five agents about the type of property they deal in, the sorts of advice given to clients on aspects of the materiality of the home, and ways of marketing it. The images of properties for sale or rent in the agent's window or advertisements in the press were used as prompts. The agents were chosen so that all inner London boroughs were represented, although the sample is not a large one.[4]

Thumbnail images courtesy of Callum Roberts.

The embedded discourses that separate people from things are implicit in agents' marketing approaches.[5] Estate agents mediate between buyers and sellers—as one agent succinctly put it, "We deal with clients not properties." The "property," as it is in agents' parlance, is the vehicle through which they earn their living either by selling it or by letting it, the latter usually for a third party—the landlord. The property is the material thing through which buyers and sellers relate in each other's absence and agents often discourage any direct relationship between the vendor and prospective purchasers.

Agents are not, by their own admission, necessarily either makers of style nor arbiters of taste but their job involves knowing how to market property. The faster the turnover of property the greater the profit for the agent since fees are usually charged only if the property sells, either as a percentage of the price fetched by the property or as a flat fee. The agent must maintain a steady flow of properties to earn a living. The location of the property, that is the area of London, is the major determining factor in the value. Within this are different types and sizes of property and then smaller gradations of value relating to the street, the "features," and condition of the actual building inside and out. The agent must be alert to and familiar with these variables in order to produce a valuation. For the vendor and the buyer the property is somewhere to dwell, and in the case of "buy to let," for tenants to inhabit, producing an income for the landlord and a fee for the managing agent.[6] For this reason the questions asked of agents in this research were about their advice to both vendors and to landlords. As property is less easy to sell in 2003 than during 2002 and 2001, agents consider the "presentation" of the property as increasingly important in effecting a swift sale.

Asked about the principal selling points of a property in their area agents listed location and nearness to transport links, neutral decorations, "the right price," large kitchens, modern kitchens, wooden floors, good bathrooms. Very few mentioned emotional reactions to property, as a factor in buying: "It's the 'X factor'—people feel at home there." Rather, for agents there are a series of material factors in the property and the problematic personalities involved. Agents dislike working for vendors who are greedy, wanting more than the market rate for their property either as a sale or a rental. Such clients are seen as a waste of resources and marketing since prices are not soaring month by month as they were in the recent past, fulfilling such ambition, and the property will fail to sell or attract tenants.

The two types of property most often categorized by the London agents interviewed are "loft apartments," either newly built or converted—often from commercial buildings—and the "period house" which constitutes a large proportion of London housing stock. Built by speculators as London grew, the latter date predominantly from the nineteenth century and early twentieth or more rarely the eighteenth century. There is also some post-Second World War housing in the London suburbs. Apart from these, almost all earlier housing was built to a similar pattern with a room to the front and back of the plot and a window in each. A stair, hall, and passage runs to one side of the plan and from this the rooms are accessed. This pattern of plan recurs regardless of the number of stories or the social class for whom it was constructed, but the ceiling heights

C.R.

and the quality of the joinery were carefully indexical of this.[7] What agents term "original features," such as fireplaces, paneled doors, picture rails, and cornices are apparently desired by many buyers of period property. Conversely the wish by buyers to replace old sash windows with plastic ones was cited as a reason to drop the price offered in some less-central areas.

The "loft apartment" is everything the period house is not, the antithesis of suburban domesticity. Developed as a type over the last twenty years in London, it ideally has none of the compartmentalized rooms but a large open reception area and kitchen combined and perhaps a split-level mezzanine area as a bedroom.[8] An apartment for rent needs one bathroom per bedroom and this is said by agents to accommodate groups of tenants desirous of each having their own bathroom. Loft apartments are increasingly marketed by area (as square feet) something rarely done for other types of property, as well as more conventionally by the number of bedrooms. In this respect and others they resemble the commercial property they once were, being in agents' accounts more knowingly "presented" by their owners, synonymous with their being more intensely commodified.

There is a further category of property and that is "ex-local authority," and in London this is most often a flat. These are generally post-Second World War although there are also earlier mansion blocks of flats built by philanthropic organizations, which later became owned by local authorities. Since the Tory government of the 1980s when council tenants were given the "right to buy" their home, these properties are now bought and sold like any other.[9] These are more variable in layout and proportionately cheaper per square foot. "Ex-local" dwellings are still marketed as "flats" whereas all other flats have become translated into "apartments" after the loft apartment.

I have sketched the spatial and material aspects of the housing types available in some detail because ideally all seemingly need to conform to the same set of desires in order to sell. That is, spaciousness, cleanliness, and neutrality. This is what buyers and tenants want according to agents. Clearly spaciousness is easiest to evoke in large rooms, which is what the loft apartment should offer, whereas the average terraced period house usually needs some adaptation to achieve this illusion.

When asked what they meant by neutral, agents listed white-, beige-, and magnolia-painted walls and, if a loft apartment or a rental,[10] a wood floor.[11] For example:

> We advise against strong colours—too much of a personal statement— neutral décor (Partner of agents in Islington, North London).

> White walls, wood floors. Neutrality sells – plainness (Agent in west central London dealing with 25–40 age group of "city types").

Neutrality is supposed to help achieve the aim of spaciousness. In many marketing photographs of reception rooms even the furniture is covered in white or neutral fabric camouflaged against the neutral wall in an effort to make it disappear and create the illusion of space.

> We tell them [the vendor] to make it look more spacey [sic], airy . . . maybe laminate flooring and mirrors, keep the curtains drawn [back]. It all helps to make it look more spacey (Sales negotiator talking about selling ex local authority flats inner East End).

> It [white] gives you a blank canvas [pause]—and most people like white anyway. My place is all painted white. Some people hire an interior designer and have pink ceilings and purple walls. You might move in and think, "I want that wall red" but then you have to sell it to someone with the same colour taste as you (Sales negotiator East London/ Docklands).

Personal taste in color is to be avoided and extreme examples were used to illustrate the point. An agent in west London related, "Colour is very individual to a particular person. For example a few years ago I had a property where one of the bedrooms was painted black . . ." This client was advised to repaint before marketing. Some agents were sensitive about offending their potential vendor's taste: "most people are quite proud of their own taste." And in south-east London:

> We had this lower ground floor flat in Peckham, a basement really and it really didn't have much light and the gentlemen had painted it bright red, right. We had it on for about a month and everyone that walked in there just walked right out again. So then we said well maybe you could paint it and he was quite happy, you know, to do that and he painted it magnolia and it sold. It's all about presentation.

The other wall surface which was mentioned as "appropriate" in apartments converted from old industrial buildings is exposed brick work. This is indexical of industry and signals the "authenticity" of the loft (Podmore 1998: 297). For example: "exposed timber beams and brickwork in this authentic riverside conversion."

Evidently there is some widely understood social consensus about neutrality. It does not mean gray, which is the color that Western color science would term neutral. Here it constitutes lightness, a feeling of space and is impersonal, a "blank canvas" in the recurring description agents give. For example an agent's promotion of an unfurnished flat to rent, '. . . an excellent opportunity for someone seeking a spacious and fresh environment in which to add their personal furnishings." Anything that is not neutral, i.e. is colored, is by implication, a personal idiosyncrasy that other people cannot relate to. Nonetheless neutrality is culturally constructed and a "fashion," just like the terracotta reds that were mentioned by agents marketing period houses as being ubiquitous a decade ago in certain areas.

Cleanliness relates to both integrity of surface and to the absence of traces of other peoples' lives. "To Live is to leave traces" wrote Walter Benjamin[12] but this is precisely what prospective buyers and tenants do not want to see, signs of others' occupation. Agents cited examples; mastic round the bath that has turned black with mildew, scuff marks on the wall, the 'tired' decorations, as signs requiring obliteration. New properties obviate the need for these erasures and agents speak admiringly of the properties that are "like show houses" in their presentation, that is, they are pristine, yet stylish—and sought after.

Unlike the Kula shell valuables of the Melanesian islands which increase in value as they are transformed from white to red by handling, or the patina on a piece of period furniture, surfaces in the contemporary home must be kept uninflected with a life lived (Campbell 1983). Or rather this is how they should be presented for sale. The analogy of Melanesian shell exchange networks is perhaps a useful one here on two further counts illuminating contrasting notions of the relationship of persons and things. The shells, exchanged in the Massim of Papua New Guinea, personify and spread the fame of the man to whom they are linked so that persons and shells are not distinct. The reddening of the shells animates them, making them materially more like persons, not only as a symbolic referent—they resemble foetuses—but also, and anthropology seldom engages with this, because of their material redness (Strathern 1999). Color is an animating presence in the world and potentially intrinsic to the fetish. Colors have different spatial qualities and red is attractive, moves forward towards the gaze. In the housing market this quality of red, for example, makes rooms appear smaller but also seems to attach the property too closely to the vendor.

Secondly, is the matter of flow, something which has been explored for the shell networks (Strathern 1996). In one of the economic arguments concerning the housing market, we are told that in order to keep that market buoyant, first-time buyers must be able to afford to enter the exchange network and keep it

C.R.

C.R.

C.R.

mobile. Without these buyers the chain will halt. Materiality though may also impede the flow or speed it up. Multiple patterned surfaces offer such an impediment. When highly patterned interiors come on to the market they considerably decrease the value of the property.

In the Marsh & Parsons particulars for "London W11," (Figure 4) for example, the need for "total refurbishment" does not mean structural problems, damp or lack of central heating, but simply the decoration, which includes the kitchen and bathroom. The highly intricate pattern animating all its surfaces, working-class taste dating perhaps from the early 1970s, makes it a recalcitrant participant in the exchange network and it is accordingly offered at a low price. This reinforces the notion of patterned surface as offering an attachment, a binding together of persons and things through their surface pattern (Gell 1998).[13] The very vitality—the "busyness" of its surfaces—offers resistance to smooth passage through the marketplace, unintentionally providing an apotropaic defense against separation from its creator (Gell 1998: 83). It offers more resistance even than the brightly colored, but plain, room. Pattern camouflages form too, pattern moving against other patterns, crowding the space.

Returning then to neutrality, an agent in central east London mentioned that some new loft apartments were more like hotel rooms and these came back on the market more frequently. Residential property differs from the impersonal nature of a hotel room, where the prerequisite is precisely never to see evidence of the previous occupant, in the care invested in it. Erasure of occupation is paradoxical in the sense that it is also taken as a sign, agents say, indicating to buyers that a property has been looked after, and is of "good quality;" this is particularly so in expensive central locations. Agents stress a moral dimension to cleanliness and presentation, for example:

> Well presented, clean tidy . . . don't leave socks and shoes lying around—or pants—then the buyer will think someone good lives here, you know it's a really emotional thing. (Senior negotiator, Notting Hill, central west London).

As property is ideally a "blank canvas" certain conventions follow in its representation in images for marketing. Thus, as is conventional in photographs of buildings in architectural magazines, estate agents' shots never contain people and are cleansed of any hint of who might live in the property.[14] Indeed, as the quote from the National Association of Estate Agents explicitly states, this is the objective. The potential buyer can only then imagine themselves inhabiting the picture. In an interior photograph in the July 2003 issue of *The London Property News*, of a "one bedroom apartment . . . offering spacious accommodation," there is a child's playpen full of toys in the reception room, a symbolic (and ironic) indication of why the occupants might want to sell such spaciousness. This picture is unusual in the intimacy revealed; mostly photographs do not depict the presence of absent people, simply absence. The rooms shown are receptive, static, composed; a domestic drama is *not* about to be enacted. There is no animation in the surfaces, no visible color or pattern except perhaps a carefully foregrounded vase of flowers. Advertisements by developers for new apartments that presently lack a material reality seem to be the only exception to this absence of persons and in these, people, usually young and glamorous, lounge on sofas—often white. Invariably the interior setting has wood floors with neutral walls.

Images of a property are important in attracting potential buyers to come and view it. These are circulated using the estate agents' shop window, website, and in advertisements in the press. One agent said: "Use a photo of a property taken on a sunny day and you get more viewings" (partner, east London). In newspaper advertisements, one photograph per property is normal whereas in an individual property's details on the Internet or from the agent's office, several are used to show different aspects. The "main selling point" is what is presented in marketing shots. Some agents use their own discretion in choosing these, while others actively consult the vendor on the rooms and on the "presentation."

Interior shots are frequently employed in expensive inner metropolitan areas and the "best feature" is chosen to represent the property. This might be the view to the outside, especially if this is of the river or spectacular in some other way. In these inner-city locations an exterior shot of the building often betrays that the interior is not a property's best feature. In Islington, central north London, where twenty years of rising property value due to proximity to the City has been applied to its housing stock, interior shots are used. These show differences in houses that agents say are essentially the same outside but have extensively individually remodeled interiors. These images are chosen to show "the wow factor" of an interior. In the outer suburbs where housing stock is also uniform, 1930s semi-detached housing for example, buyers are shown only the front of the house and perhaps the garden; it is from this information that they can choose the age and style of the property, while the interiors are all more or less similar.

ANY COLOR SO LONG AS IT'S WHITE

The more expensive the area—St Johns Wood and Notting Hill, for example—the more likely people are to replace bathrooms especially, and kitchens. There seems to be a "because they can" element in this, agents citing with pride the style and wealth of their clients who can afford to have what they want.

> They often change the property as soon as they move in, they know what's new, what's contemporary. They don't like carpets. Most of our clients are city workers and are very controlled [sic] i.e. they know what they want" (Sales negotiator, City).

The bathrooms and kitchen were repeatedly mentioned by letting agents as making or breaking a rental in central London. For property that has rental potential—loft apartments and ex-local-authority flats—the kitchen and its equipment is crucial to attracting tenants. The property might then be valued as it is or with a new kitchen, giving the vendor the choice—the profit, or lack of it, to be made.

In outer suburban locations the kitchen is an important factor, more so than the bathroom. Emphasized by agents here as an expensive purchase, a "modern" kitchen already installed therefore made a property more valuable and saleable. Conversely new bathroom suites, agents said, don't cost a great deal of money and so long as a bathroom is "well presented," an old colored suite did not have to devalue the place. Certain types of older terraced period housing originally built without a bathroom often have these attached to the kitchen on the ground floor, since this is where the plumbing and drainage is already located. This layout is against the prevailing ideal of multiple accessible (preferably "en-suite") bathrooms and modern (and therefore white) expensive fittings are needed to counteract its devaluing effect.

In central London few agents selling houses rather than potentially tenanted flats, said they advised clients to fit new kitchens in order to sell a property because it is in kitchens that personal taste is exercised. Installing a new kitchen is one of the ways the purchaser marks their own taste. An agent in south London told how he remembered a particular vendor who was, the agent thought, inordinately proud of his kitchen. The implication was that the kitchen, with its solid oak cupboards and the nuances of taste and value it represented to the owner, was far too expensive for the type of house in this location and would be lost on potential buyers who are "on a budget," as he put it:

> Kitchens are very, very personal, often it's not worth putting in a new one because people have such different taste in kitchens. I've learnt not to say anything because you never know what taste people will have and you've put the idea in their head then (Sales negotiator, Greenwich, South London).

We would advise redecoration in this market as it's tougher than last year. But for sale no, I wouldn't advise upgrading the kitchen or bathroom because people like to make their mark on them (the place) themselves . . . Brits especially like to go to Homebase.[15] There are so many different kitchens on the market now—brushed steel is not everyone's cup of tea (Partner, central east London).

The brand of the appliances also indicates distinction (Bourdieu 1984).

The bathroom and kitchen are very important in terms of gauging the rest of the apartment. For example if there's a Miele hob that indicates quality but if it's an AEG hob or Whirlpool washing machine . . . (Manager, St Johns Wood, north-west London).

These latter two brands are apparently not expensive enough to index "quality" nor show the financial status of the vendor in a favorable light, indicating perhaps that the buyer likes to identify the vendor as someone like him.

Although many agents said people wanted have to a bathroom in their own taste, this is exercised within narrow parameters which involve whiteness. In upmarket areas and loft apartments the fittings must not be "reproduction" either. An avocado or pink bathroom suite is said to devalue the property although a potential buyer may find this appealing if the price is right, in that it can be ripped out with impunity and replaced to suit her own taste. Although two agents suggested that white bathroom suites were also, like the pink and avocado, a "fashion," these latter are fashions from the past and therefore indicate that the bathroom is not new, but is—a word that recurs frequently—"tired." Since new bathroom suites are almost invariably white, personal taste is exercised in the brand of the suite, taps, shower, and in the wall and floor finishes. Distinction rests in the cost and branding of appliances, taps, and fittings.

At the moment I see a lot of those sand coloured tiles, you know like you get in a five star hotel—at least I saw them in a five star hotel in Dubai—and Phillipe Stark taps and Grohe showerheads (Senior sales negotiator, central west London).

An agent in Catford, a less-expensive suburb of south London, suggested that good tiles and lighting meant that people would not notice a cheap bathroom or kitchen. It was all, he added, a matter of presentation.

When showing potential buyers round the property, it is undesirable for the vendor to be there, particularly in small flats because, like too much furniture, he clutters up the place, making it appear less spacious. Vendors often shoot themselves in the foot by talking too much about their property. If buyers are now able to spend more time viewing a property than in times of hectic market activity, it is still a very brief interlude for a purchase so large. Buyers searching in outer suburbs seem to spend slightly longer looking, perhaps two half-hour visits, before making an offer for the property as against two visits of ten to twenty minutes reported by the agents working in central London.[16]

During the last few years in the UK a raft of new television programs has appeared on the subject of home decoration. These are of broadly two kinds: firstly the design approach in various formats, such as the "makeover" show where someone's home or garden is transformed in a miraculously short space of time by neighbors and/or the TV team. Secondly the home as commodity—how to become a property developer, how to make your property more desirable to buyers. Asked if television programs had made their job easier, agents almost all said yes. Such exposure had increased awareness of presentation, alerting people to the potential value in their home—of "how their home should look." "People are more aware of presentation—they can make more money as well as enjoy it (their house)" (Partner, south east London). One agent in west London remarked, "People seem to think that if they paint a wall white it'll get them another 15 grand. Presentation increases saleability but not price. There's a market cap for that type of property and that's it."

CONSTRUCTING NEUTRALITY

Neutrality is hard work to achieve and unforgiving to maintain, in that patina, synonymous with "tiredness" is the undesirable result of failure to "look after" or of large tracts of time passing. Pale, quietly colored decoration is not just indexical of the home as commodity but also embodies it. The neutrality is a backdrop for the accessories or fit-outs it supports, most notably the kitchen and bathroom. An agent in Docklands (east London) dealing only in loft apartments, placed location as always the most important factor in sale and value because, "You can always improve a property but you can't move it." Like commercial office space, often refitted for each new leaseholder, the partitioning of its area and the materiality of its fittings are disposable. It is not a fixed place, only a location and can be remade afresh each time. But even then the resulting fit-out has to be "neutral" although the materials may differ from the merely fashionable—wood flooring—to the "cutting edge"—waxed concrete, say. To do otherwise risks devaluing the property. Within such strict constraints (white bathroom suite, chrome fittings) lies the distinction of taste and wealth. Obviously, the more expensive the square footage, the more prestigious it is to own a large amount of it. But the illusion of space can be created. The owners of even small flats must aim to achieve the appearance of spaciousness.

The "blank canvas" nature of walls of beige, white, magnolia or cream, minimizes their material presence. Even the exposed brick work of the authentic loft, though it is perhaps structural or symbolizes structure, is neutralized and part of the decorative effect. Despite the proclivity for depth ontology displayed in the Western tradition, surface is what is important and as Wigley writes, "Much of the complexity . . . (of the discourse around modern architecture) derives from its privileging of the surface" (Wigley 1995: 352). What agents say resonates with architect and self-publicist Le Corbusier's theoretical dressing of whiteness eighty years ago, dissected so tellingly by Wigley in *White Walls Designer Dresses*. In the critical discourses of modern architecture, white surfaces first become "natural" and then gradually become just surfaces, all references to their colors ceasing. Whiteness has become a "given" of modernist history even though many canonical modernist buildings including those by Corbusier had highly colored surfaces, albeit in colors justified as rational, scientific and disciplined. Measuring color and producing models to standardize it was part of a wider systematization using three dimensions, hue, saturation, and brightness, which is still used by paint manufacturers (among many others) and came into being during the end of the nineteenth century and the start of the twentieth, a gradual accretion of culturally constructed ideas (van Brakel 2002). At the point of its sale or rent, color is too personal, too emotive, and too problematic and can only mar the product, making it appear unnatural and *irrational* compared with the socially acceptable, genderless, given currency of neutrality, as well as producing the unfortunate effect of binding the property to its vendor.

Housing is not marketed on the basis of its solid structure or replete insulation but on its decorative qualities. Housing is then, in Wigley's interpolation of Semper, "an effect of decoration," although not of the sort that Semper had in mind (Wigley 1995: 11). Wigley traces the link between fashion, gender, and architecture, between a structure and its cladding, as evinced successively by Gottfried Semper, Adolf Loos, and Le Corbusier, through the relationship of a material and its dressing. Semper eulogized the primitive use of patterned textiles as cladding to a structure; it is this cladding as ornament that produces architecture, the decoration is the clothing and the coat of paint recapitulates the earlier textile. In the *Law of Dressing* first published in 1898 Loos, influenced by Semper, drew parallels between dress on the human body and the dressing of built structure. He desires that there be no confusion between a material and its dressings—the dressings must not simulate the material they cover. Loos famously decried "ornament as crime," as a predilection of savage, uncivilized man. The cladding takes the place of ornament but is still, as in Semper's analysis, distinct from structure, liberated from it. (The recent widespread installation of laminate, imitation wood flooring over wooden floorboards would

C.R.

for example, be an anathema to Loos.) As Wigley puts it, the coat of paint is the paradigm. Loos parallels the design of clothing with that of architecture, but he rejects fashion in clothing as feminine, too sensual and like ornament, while men's dress in the form of suits is rational, functional, standardized, and inconspicuous. Corbusier uses the simile of the man's well-cut suit and his white shirt as appropriate, discreet, and moral covers for nakedness and for the well-tailored building (Wigley 1995). Whiteness as hygiene, or the look of hygiene that is to be found in Corbusier, has its roots in earlier European history. Deploring any but white surfaces, Corbusier writes ". . . stains do not show on the medley of our damasks and patterned wall papers" (Wigley 1995: 8).

This taste for neutrality in contemporary London fulfills Corbusier's early manifesto for whiteness, "The Law of Ripolin." As anyone who has painted a bare plaster wall—pinkish beige or gray—will know, white walls do not make a room look bigger, only brighter. White makes the walls appear to come forward but light bouncing off them makes the room bright. For Corbusier, says Wigley, whereas colored walls can structure it, a white wall does not adjust space at all, one surface becomes indistinguishable from another, "the neutrality of white is understood as a neutrality from space itself" (Wigley 1995: 217). The blackened junction of bath and wall cited by the agent above as drawing the eye and requiring erasure, interrupts the seamless flow of surfaces in the room. The moldy mastic has become matter out of place, literally as well as symbolically violating boundaries (Douglas 1966: 35). There are also echoes of Corbusier and Semper in the moral aspect of neutral decoration and in the notion that surfaces should create a space rather than be in it. The lack of color is an interpretation of modernism that owes much to later critical discourse. Agents do not mention neutral decoration in sales literature, except perhaps for rentals, because—in loft apartments in particular—it is a given, just as the white-painted wall was a given in the received construct of mid twentieth century modernism. But images, and words such as "spacious," "bright," and "light" show that neutral walls are present.

It is in the effect of the material surfaces of the building that its agency lies. Even if there are colored areas in the property they will be shown in the marketing images only if there is no other choice. Surface neutrality is not just the look of modernism or "minimalism," it is also the look of the dwelling as commodity in its presentation to the market. The building's surfaces are relieved of the detritus of lived life, of social life, and exhibited in an ahistorical present as unadulterated surface. If owners do dare to express themselves, other than through gradated neutral materials—"wood" laminate for rentals and less-expensive family housing, timber floors, limestone tiles, etc.—they risk losing money on their largest capital investment. But this is the agent's tale, not the vendor's, where presentation is also representation. The insight that "The perception of space is not what space is but one of its representations; in this sense built space has no more authority than drawings, photographs, or descriptions," might refer to the circulated images of a property (Colomina 1992: 75). The representation of the materiality of the property as neutral embodies its status as a commodity. And yet the obsession with neutral decoration is itself fetishistic, as betrayed in the remark of the west London estate agent cited above; the expectation by the vendor that a coat of white paint will magically attract more money.

A property can be *too* neutral, too "like a hotel room" and this too will slow its passage as an item of exchange. It must exhibit at the time of sale, the right amount of personal expression—residing in furniture and fittings—and especially in the "accessories" of kitchens and bathrooms. In a linkage evoking Loos, property can be "dressed" to sell, described by an agent in north London of his own house, recently sold, as using fluffy white bathroom towels, plants, cut flowers, cushions, throws. The kitchen and bathroom fittings are also, I suggest, the "dressing" in Loos's sense. Since modernism, becoming inseparable from functionalism, was to transcend fashion, its theorists eschewed any similarity of buildings to clothing—and thus to persons (Wigley 1995).[17]

A recent film called *The Delapidated Dwelling*[18] deplored the state of the UK's period housing stock, comparing it to the sophisticated electronic technology that dominates other aspects of life. Can housing as a trick of decoration be justified if it does not respond to heat, cold, noise, rain? Housing with walls one brick thick is inadequate however gorgeous its bathroom(s) and kitchen. It is not though for its qualities of insulation that a property is in general either valued or desired in the contemporary London property market. Only one agent remembered that "in the 1980s and early '90s people asked about insulation but not now."[19] It is for its look, for the illusion of spaciousness, cleanliness, and blandness of interior surfaces of its one brick thick neutrality that it realizes most money. Its decoration is disconnected from its structure in the way that Semper idealized, but not quite because instead the structure has migrated into the neutral interior walls, even the neutral furniture, and the "dressing" is in the kitchen, bathroom(s), and "accessories." The actual structure and fabric of the property has become almost a tedious irrelevance. Neutral decoration then, equipped with the appropriate dressings, presents no resistance to sale, whereas its opposite, the patterned interior where every surface ensnares with its animation is "intractable and peculiar" and does not move through the exchange process with ease (Strathern 1999: 192).

CONCLUSION

In this article I have explored the material agency of the property at its point of consumption. We would have to know the buyer's and the vendor's tale to know the full story, how much for example, property is being "done up" for the purpose of selling (cf. Clarke 2001). The neutral flexible interior might be paralleled to the postmodern theorizing of the self as fluid and adaptable (e.g. Giddens 1991). But it also tells us more about the relationship between persons and things and of the commodity and the fetish. The distinction—and the necessity of this—between people and things that is manifested by the neutrality represented in the agents' marketing tools, is opposed to the highly colored or patterned dwelling whose surfaces adhere property and person (vendor) to one another.

Baudrillard remarks that the world of color is opposed to the world of value, "the bourgeois interior reduces it for the most part to discreet tints and 'shades'" (1986: 31). The bourgeois taste for discreet decoration is perhaps also an expansion of the need to control and order objects, a fear, in short, of the oppressive personification of things. Neutrality subdues a building, makes it passive, tranquil, undemanding, hovering on the brink of disappearance, embodying a socially constructed rationality. Only the householder's personal "dressings" endow it with vitality, whereas the highly patterned interior disguises dirt and threatens to engulf with its tightly animated surfaces. There is no guarantee that these objects do not have a secret life, no guarantee that the house itself is not alive, and the furniture dancing while the inhabitants sleep.

In the Papuan shell exchanges reddening creates value and further animates the shells, adding to their fetishistic power as things that can become persons. In the London housing market, the *lack* of bright color or pattern creates value and is a prerequisite of commodification. To return to Marx, the house becomes evacuated of usefulness and materiality, and is reduced only to its exchange value (Stallybrass 1998). For Marx, although the commodity takes the shape of a physical thing, the "commodity form" has no relation to the physical nature of the commodity and the material relations arising out of this (Stallybrass 1998: 184). It does seem, however, that in the case of London property discussed in this article, the "commodity form" echoes the physical nature of the commodity itself. As commodity, the neutral property is emptied out of "particularity and thingliness." Yet agency is embodied in the specific materiality of things, in this case their color, which structures the creation of space, the creation of value, and influences the attachment between people and objects.

ACKNOWLEDGMENTS

This article was researched during the period of an ESRC Postdoctoral Fellowship Award number T026271266, at the Department of Anthropology, University College London. Thanks to Alison Clarke, Victor Buchli, and two anonymous

Figure 1
Image courtesy of
Stirling Ackroyd.

Figure 2
Image courtesy of
Stirling Ackroyd.

Figure 3
Image courtesy of GMV.

Marsh & Parsons

Established 1856

Residential Sales & Acquisitions
Residential Lettings
Commercial
Property Management
Professional Services
Lettings Management & Refurbishment

London, W11

An unmodernised ex local authority flat in need of total refurbishment located on the third floor within a 1950's block situated in this highly desirable crescent. The property offers an excellent investment opportunity. The property benefits from a locakble storage cupboard situated outside the front door.

3 Bedrooms: Reception Room: Kitchen: Bathroom: Guest WC: Communal

Gardens

£325,000 Leasehold Subject to Contract

Measurements are approximate and no responsibility is taken for any error, omission or mis-statement in these particulars which do not constitute an offer or contract. No representation or warranty whatever is made or given either during negotiations, in particulars or elsewhere.

Notting Hill Office: 020 7313 2890

marshandparsons.co.uk

Figure 4
Image courtesy of Marsh and Parsons, 4–6 Kensington Park Road, London W11 3BU, UK.

Figure 5
Image courtesy of
Stirling Ackroyd.

Figure 6
Images courtesy of Proprium
Estates Ltd.

reviewers for their helpful comments and suggestions. The resulting article is of course my responsibility.

NOTES

1. Anyone can set themselves up as an estate agent but there are various regulatory bodies of which the largest is the National Association of Estate Agents. It is possible to buy and sell property privately without estate agents but this is still a minority of property transactions in the UK. See Palm and Daniels (2002) for a US study of internet property sales.
2. Source: Government Office for London 2003
3. Source: Government Office for London 2003. At the 2001 census there were 1,219,859 households in inner London (Source: Office of National Statistics). Historically inner London has had low owner-occupier households and high rentals, something now reversed (Buck et al. 2002: 157).
4. The agents were each interviewed once during July and August 2003; the summer holiday period is always considered a quiet time of year for the housing market. Only two of the agents contacted were reluctant to take part. These were employed by chains of high-street estate agents whose policy was to refer me to their public relations representatives. I did not interview these representatives.
5. Prospective buyers may of course have a very different view from the agent of what they are looking for in a dwelling, hinted at by an agent reporting that some buyers liked to talk to the vendor at length, "you'd think they were buying the people" perhaps indicating a personification of the house.
6. The "buy to let" phenomenon has been extensively discussed and publicized in the UK. The explanation given for its efflorescence is an economic one although doubtless other factors were and are at play. The low interest rates on mortgages and the month-by-month acceleration of housing prices combining to make property an attractive investment yielding better returns than the ailing stock market. By 2003 there was, according to the agents interviewed, an oversupply of rental accommodation in London and the price accelerations had ceased although interest rates remained low. Agents reported that many people who had bought one extra property—most usually a one or two bedroom flat—were now selling this, while "professional" landlords were still "looking to acquire."
7. A grander variation is the "double fronted" house where the plan is symmetrical about the hallway. See for example Long (1993) on the Edwardian house and Summerson (1978) on the Georgian, also Porter (2000) for a broader social history of the capital.
8. See Zukins (1982) on the original SoHo lofts of Manhattan and Podmore (1998) for a study of loft apartments in Montreal. The new-build London apartment now bears only nodding acquaintance with its original open plan, big space template, something agents volunteered in this research.
9. See assessments such as Dolan (1999: 70): Thatcher's "'property owning democracy' . . . emphasis(ed) ownership and nation rather than selling" and Hall and Jacques (1989).
10. I.e. landlords required this as tenants demanded it.
11. Two agents marketing loft apartments in the central area, both describing their marketing as "at the cutting edge," reported that in their newest recently completed lofts, limestone or granite tiles were replacing wood. These materials are still "neutral" in effect, albeit indexing expensive and distinctive neutrality.
12. Used as the opening in Colomina (1992).
13. See especially pp. 74–95 on pattern. Gell has no interest in color per se.
14. Although it is arguable that architects are interested in gleaning information about the materiality of buildings, not their commodification; people detract from the aesthetics. The building is here detached from its social use.
15. Homebase is one of a number of high-street DIY stores in the UK.

16. A property is marketed at a certain "asking" price and a prospective buyer makes an "offer" mediated by the agent.
17. Wigley's target here is the influential modernist commentator Seigfreid Gideon.
18. Patrick Keiller, 2000. Illuminations.
19. It is in the survey, carried out by a qualified surveyor, whose report is usually a condition of the mortgage that such details might emerge as agents pointed out, but insulation is not a marketing factor for most property.

REFERENCES

Attfield, Judy. 1999. "Bringing Modernity Home." In Irene Cieraad (ed.) *At Home: An Anthropology of Domestic Space*, pp. 73–82. New York: Syracuse University Press.

Baudrillard, Jean. 1996 [1968]. *The System of Objects*, trans. James Benedict. London and New York: Verso.

Bourdieu, Pierre. 1984. *Distinction: A Social Critique of the Judgement of Taste*. London: Routledge and Kegan Paul.

van Brakel, Jaap. 2002. "The Coming into being of Colour Spaces." In Barbara Saunders and Jaap van Brakel (eds) *Theories Technologies Instrumentalities of Color. Anthropological and Historiographic Perspectives*, pp. 305–25. University of America Press.

Buck, N., Ian Gordon, Peter Hall, Michael Harlow and Mark Kleinman. 2002. *Working Capital: Life and Labour in Contemporary Britain*. Routledge, London.

Campbell, S. 1983. "Attaining Rank: A Classification of Shell Valuables." In J. Leach and E. Leach (eds) *The Kula*, pp. 229–49. Cambridge: Cambridge University Press.

Clarke, Alison J. 2001. "The Aesthetics of Social Aspiration." In Daniel Miller (ed.) *Home Possessions*, pp. 23–45. Oxford: Berg..

Colomina, Beatriz (ed.). 1992. "The Split Wall: Domestic Voyeurism." In *Sexuality and Space*, pp. 73–131. Princeton, NJ: Princeton Architectural Press.

Conway, J. 1984. *Capital Decay. An Analysis of London's Housing*. London: SHAC.

Dolan, John A. 1999. "I've Always Fancied Owning me Own Lion." In Irene Cieraad (ed.) *At Home: An Anthropology of Domestic Space*, pp. 60–72. New York: Syracuse University Press.

Douglas, Mary. 1966. *Purity and Danger: An Analysis of Concepts of Pollution and Taboo*. London: Routledge and Kegan Paul.

Giddens, Anthony. 1991. *Modernity and Self-identity: Self and Society in the Late Modern Age*. Cambridge: Polity Press in association with Basil Blackwell.

Gell, Alfred. 1998. *Art and Agency. An Anthropological Theory*. Oxford: Clarendon Press.

Hall, Stuart and Martin Jacques (eds). 1989. *New Times: The Changing Face of Politics in the 1990s*. London: Lawrence & Wishart in association with *Marxism Today*.

Long, Helen C. 1993. *The Edwardian House*. Manchester and New York: Manchester University Press.

Miller, Daniel. 1990. "Appropriating the State on the Council Estate." In Tim Putman and Charles Newton (eds) *Household Choices*, pp. 43–55. London: Future Publications.

Miller, Daniel (ed.). 2001a. *Home Possessions*. Oxford: Berg.

Miller, Daniel (ed.). 2001b. "Possessions." In *Home Possessions*, pp. 107–22. Oxford: Berg.

Palm, R. and M. Daniels 2002. "The Internet and Home Purchase." *Tijdschrift voor economische en sociale geographie* 93(5), 537–47.

Podmore, Julie. 1998. "(Re)reading the 'Loft Living' Habitus in Montréal's Inner City." *International Journal of Urban and Regional Research* 22(2), 283–302.

Porter, Roy. 2000. *London: A Social History*. London: Penguin.

Spyer, Patricia (ed.). 1998. "Introduction." In *Border Fetishisms: Material Objects in Unstable Spaces*, pp. 1–12. London and New York: Routledge.

Stallybrass, Peter. 1998. "Marx's Coat." In Patricia Spyer (ed.) *Border Fetishisms: Material Objects in Unstable Spaces*, pp. 183–207. London and New York: Routledge.

Strathern, M. 1996. "Cutting the Network." *Journal of the Royal Anthropological Institute* 2(3), 517–35.

Strathern, M. 1999. *Property Substance and Effect: Anthropological Essays on Persons and Things*. London and New Jersey: Athlone Press.

Summerson, John. 1978. *Georgian London*. Harmondsworth: Penguin.

Wigley, Mark. 1995. *White Walls Designer Dresses*. London and Cambridge, MA: MIT Press.

Zukin, S. 1982. *Loft Living: Culture and Capital in Urban Change*. Baltimore, MD: Johns Hopkins University Press.

HOME CULTURES   VOLUME 1, ISSUE 1.   REPRINTS AVAILABLE   PHOTOCOPYING   © BERG 2004
PP 23–50   DIRECTLY FROM THE   PERMITTED BY LICENSE   PRINTED IN THE UK
PUBLISHERS.   ONLY

ANKE VAN CAUDENBERG AND HILDE HEYNEN

THE RATIONAL KITCHEN IN THE INTERWAR PERIOD IN BELGIUM: DISCOURSES AND REALITIES[1]

ANKE VAN CAUDENBERG
GRADUATED IN 2002 AS A
MASTER OF SCIENCE IN
ENGINEERING:
ARCHITECTURE AT THE
KATHOLIEKE UNIVERSITEIT
LEUVEN (BELGIUM).

HILDE HEYNEN IS PROFESSOR
OF ARCHITECTURAL THEORY
AT THE KATHOLIEKE
UNIVERSITEIT LEUVEN
(BELGIUM). SHE IS THE
AUTHOR OF *ARCHITECTURE
AND MODERNITY. A CRITIQUE*
AND CO-EDITED, WITH
HUBERT-JAN HENKET, *BACK
FROM UTOPIA. THE
CHALLENGE OF THE MODERN
MOVEMENT.*

Modernist architects introduced the rational kitchen to Belgium from 1930 onwards. The influence of the CIAM (Congrés Internationaux d'Architecture Moderne/International Congresses of Modern Architecture) discourse on the rational minimum dwelling was clearly visible, in architects' journals as well as in women's magazines. The most important Belgian contribution to the further development of the rational kitchen was the CUBEX kitchen, a design by Louis-Herman De Koninck of standardized cupboard items that could be combined in different ways. This system was to become a huge commercial success, and has been installed in thousands of Belgian kitchens, before as well as after the

Second World War. The reception of the architects' discourse on the rational kitchen, however, was different among the different social strata. Whereas bourgeois and middle-class women in general applauded the new ideas about kitchen design and the appliances that went with it, the climate among rural and working-class women was far less receptive. Magazines aimed at these strata of women almost ignored the matter, or confined themselves to a few off-hand suggestions as to the facilitation of household tasks by special techniques or tools. Consistently, the workmen's housing built between 1925 and 1940 did not apply the rational kitchen, the argument being that a limited budget did not allow for it. New housing for the middle classes and the bourgeois apartments, on the other hand, were the contexts where rational kitchens were most successfully applied.

INTRODUCTION

In 1929 Angéline Japsenne, Secretary General of the Belgian Ligues ouvrières féminines chrétiennes (Christian Female Workers Guilds), attended a congress in Frankfurt, organized by the CIAM (Congrès Internationaux d'Architecture Moderne/International Congresses of Modern Architecture)[2] on the topic of Die Wohnung für das Existenzminimum—the minimum standard dwelling.[3] She reported about this experience in a contribution to her organization's periodical, entitled "La maison 'minimum'" (Japsenne 1929). She appeared to be quite impressed by the architects' discourse on the necessity to introduce new dwelling plans that were rational and comfortable, with a layout that provided:

> day-, night- and service-rooms, arranged in such a way that they are easy to maintain and agreeable to live in; a small kitchen, but equipped in such a practical way that the most common tasks can be properly done; . . . (Japsenne 1929: 534).[4]

Japsenne's Frankfurt experience and her reporting of it were part of a campaign on proper ways of living, launched by the Ligue with the objective of training working-class women in household skills. The Minimum Dwelling, as proposed by the CIAM, was seen by her as a very useful tool to further this goal:

> [The Minimum Dwelling] indeed means a considerable step towards the solution of a problem which always was of major concern to us: the acquisition, by the working class, of attractive homes, healthy, provided with all the amenities made available by the actual progress of technology (Japsenne 1930: 580).[5]

A good dwelling, however, would only be really useful when the inhabitants lived in it in an appropriate manner. Therefore the families, mainly the women, had to be taught how to arrange their home, and principally the kitchen, according to a more rational conception.

> The first thing necessary is the arranging of a kitchen, where domestic tasks can be exerted in a hygienic way, causing a normal fatigue of the housewife, and not an exhaustion their nature does not justify (Japsenne 1930: 582).[6]

Japsenne deplored the fact that, in 1930, there was not yet a kitchen available on the market that was really rational and cheap enough to be affordable to the majority of people. She pleaded with the architects to devote their energies to the design of the equipped kitchen, adding the request: "But please, Sirs architects, consult the housewives before making your plans!" (Japsenne 1930: 582).[7]

Japsenne's presence in Frankfurt shows that rational housekeeping was at the time a major issue in women's organizations. In some European countries, modernist architects worked closely together with specialists in domestic economy, in order to develop rational kitchen plans. The rationalization of domestic work—known also as domestic economy (nineteenth century) or "taylorisation"[8] of the household (twentieth century)—had been introduced by American women in the second half of the nineteenth century, and came to Europe after the First World War. The intention was to make it possible for the housewife to save money, time, and effort in performing domestic tasks, by means of efficient working methods and appropriate design, equipment and organization of the home. As a result, women would be able to fulfill properly their important social role as homemaker and guardian of family stability, and, by consequence, improve the stability of society as a whole.

Germany was at the front line of developing the rational kitchen in Europe. Especially in Frankfurt, where Ernst May was directing a major social housing effort, the design of a standard built-in kitchen received ample attention. Grethe Schütte-Lihotzky[9] designed in 1926 the famous and well-documented Frankfurt kitchen, in cooperation with German household experts. In 1927 the kitchen for the workers' houses designed by J.J.P. Oud for the Stuttgart Weissenhofsiedlung—a demonstration project promoting new modern architecture—was devoped in close collaboration with Erna Meyer, the author of *Der neue Haushalt* (*The New Household*) (Hoste 1928; Seroen 1928). In the Netherlands (Bervoets 1998; Cieraad 1998), England (Darling 2000), and France (Segalen 1994) similar crossovers between experts in home economics and architects have been documented and studied.

In this article we intend to investigate the dealings with the rational kitchen in Belgium, in architectural discourse as well as in women's magazines and in built reality. We pay attention to these different fields because we want to understand how and where ideas concerning the rational kitchen were developed, how they were received as part of normative discourses on dwelling, and how they were put into practice in the actual construction of different kinds of housing.[10]

THE RATIONALIZATION OF THE KITCHEN IN ARCHITECTURAL DISCOURSE

Although several Belgian architects were closely associated with the CIAM,[11] their active interest in the topic of the rational kitchen emerged only after they became informed about the latest developments by their attendance at the Frankfurt CIAM Congress of 1929 (Bourgeois 1930). The Belgian version of the rationalization of the kitchen thus was rather simillar to those in other countries, such as Germany and the Netherlands. Belgian architects were as convinced as their foreign colleagues that the rationalization of the kitchen would help the housewife to properly fulfill her major role in the family and hence in society. The kitchen was considered the pivot of domestic activities, the place where the housewife spent most of her time and put in most of her efforts. Maurice Gaspards, for example, stated in a 1933 issue of *Bâtir*, the most influential architectural periodical of the time:

> In the home, the kitchen is the room where the equipment ought to be studied with the greatest precision. The aim should be to create a practical framework where the housewife stays an important part of her days; to the detriment of her health if the problem is badly solved (Gaspard 1933: 146).[12]

Saving time, money and effort by rationalizing the kitchen was of great importance. Louis-Herman De Koninck, one of the best-known Belgian modern architects, agreed that: "by arranging a kitchen in a rational manner, the most important goal is achieved: household work is facilitated, health increases and the housewife's well-being is enhanced" (De Koninck 1933: 736).[13]

In order to reach these goals, a modern architect should be an expert at the "art of housekeeping" and had to be well informed about the equipment of the kitchen.

Just like their foreign colleagues, Belgian architects referred to the principles of scientific housekeeping to obtain an efficient kitchen layout. Several articles written by modern architects in different journals testify to their systematic approach to the subject (De Koninck 1931; Gilles 1931; Henrotin 1932a, b, c, 1933). First, they set out to determine the different activities in the kitchen and to group activities that belonged together.[14] Secondly, they arranged those activity centers in a logical order to minimize necessary movements and to arrive at a rational plan requiring the minimum of steps between different activities. One of the most elaborate examples of such a plan is presented by Claire-Lucille Henrotin, a woman architect who graduated from the modernist La Cambre school (Figure 1 and 2).[15]

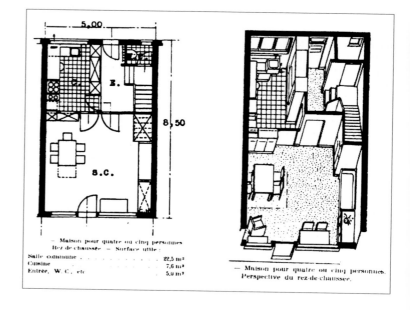

Figure 1
Floor plan and perspective of a home organized in an appropriate way (according to C.-L. Henrotin 1932).

Figure 2
Plan of a rational kitchen for a family with about five family members (Henrotin 1933).

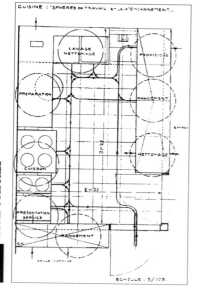

Most Belgian architects who had an opinion on the matter professed, much like their German and Dutch colleagues, a preference for the separate work-kitchen. Henrotin, for example clearly argued in favor of this type of kitchen:

> provide next to the living space, a small kitchen where the housewife has near at hand everything, arranged according to a well studied plan, that is necessary to prepare a meal. Only the kitchen conceived like this deserves the title of rational kitchen (Henrotin 1932a: 25).[16]

Like Grethe Schütte-Lihotzky, Henrotin discerned four different kitchen-types— "living-kitchen," "alcove-kitchen," "dining-kitchen," and "work-kitchen." She indicated that she preferred the "work-kitchen," for bringing together the majority of the domestic activities in one separate room and safeguarding the rest of the house against hindrances such as smells and noises. In order to optimize the required efforts of the housewife, an efficient and logical placing of this "work-kitchen" in relation with the other rooms was necessary. According to Henrotin the kitchen was to be situated next to the dining room (or the dining corner in the living room) and needed to have a direct connection with the hall or with outside. In order to facilitate keeping an eye on the children, she proposed a transparent door or partition. She organized the kitchen in accordance with a laboratory layout, as an architectural translation of the principles of the scientific household, opting for built-in equipment and a rational storing of all the utensils (Henrotin 1932c).

Whereas the Belgian rationalization of the kitchen was in many respects very similar to that in neighboring countries, its specificity was in its dealings with efficient cupboards. Huib Hoste, a prominent modernist, argued in 1937:

It's striking how nowadays one discusses no longer the kitchen layout, but rather the kitchen equipment. Whereas the layout consists of the correct placing of sink and cooker, this can still be inefficient in case the housewife hasn't near at hand beside sink and cooker all the necessary household goods. One should therefore equip the kitchen with the necessary fixed cupboards, in each case conceived and appropriate for what they have to store (Hoste 1937: 77).[17]

A good kitchen layout was important, but would not be really functional until the kitchen cabinets were practical too. In 1931 De Koninck stressed that furniture was the regulator of coordination within housekeeping (De Koninck 1931). The dimensions of kitchen furniture should be optimally tuned to the (female) human scale, so one should not have to take more steps than necessary. In addition, the kitchen utensils had to be stored and ordered in a rational manner—"a place for everything and everything in its place"—since, according to C.-L. Henrotin:

If the first condition to be fulfilled by the room serving as kitchen is to allow a logical disposition of the furniture, then this, for his part, has to be rational, has to facilitate and as it were automate the rational arrangement of all the utensils required by the different kitchen tasks (Henrotin 1932c: 51).[18]

To realize all this, fixed, built-in furniture was considered essential because the cupboards could then be entirely integrated in the concept of the kitchen and optimally tuned to their purpose. Another advantage was that alterations by the inhabitants, that could affect the good arrangement, were made impossible (Henrotin 1932b).

Apart from the fact that the furniture should be built-in, it was stressed that it had to be composed of standardized elements. Standardization was considered very important because: "if one has to manufacture special furniture for each separate case, then the cost price per unit will be very high. So, one should come to a serial production by means of standardisation" (Henrotin 1932c: 51).[19] By means of serial production of a selected number of basic modules that could be composed in many different ways, all families should be able to enjoy affordable efficient kitchen equipment. The rational kitchen would then become affordable as well as adaptable to everyone's wishes.

It is indeed in the realm of kitchen furniture that Belgium has rightfully gained a reputation: the standardized CUBEX cupboard elements, created by L.-H. De Koninck, have been very successful and have given many families the opportunity to compose the kitchen of their dreams. The equipment of the CUBEX kitchen was introduced to the public at the third CIAM Congress in Brussels in 1930. It consisted of a kitchen composed of standardized elements—four cupboard types that could be arranged in ten different ways—that allowed for 200 different kitchen models. Although it was presented as collectively designed by the Belgian CIAM group (CIAMB), the plans were clearly drawn by L. H. De Koninck (Ruëgg 1989: 204). Since De Koninck had had the opportunity to investigate in detail the "semi-industrialised" Frankfurter Küche (during CIAM II in Frankfurt), he had been increasingly interested in built-in furniture. In his opinion, the disadvantage of the Frankfurt kitchen equipment was its lack of universality:

Despite the qualities and the great number of homes, I'm of the opinion that due to the loss of universality the problem did not receive a perfect solution. Each kitchen consists of only 3 or 4 elements and the architects can therefore apply only a limited variety of layouts.[20]

Convinced that standardization and rationalization could be further enhanced, he developed an adaptable system of kitchen cupboards that could be arranged in many different ways. The CIAMB convinced the industrialist E. J. Van de Ven[21] to produce the kitchen cupboards. In 1931 Van de Ven and the CIAMB signed the contract and the trademark "CUBEX" became registered (Ruëgg 1989: 209). The CUBEX kitchen provided a remarkable success story, for it found great favor with the public. From 1931 till 1960, an impressive quantity of newly built houses and apartments were equipped with CUBEX kitchens, and the CIAMB used the yields of their royalties to finance the activities of the CIAMB (Van Loo and Zampa 1994: 211–12). In 1938, CUBEX was even marketed in Britain under the name "CUBAX." The major success of the CUBEX kitchen is largely due to the great amount of promotional activity performed by Van de Ven. CUBEX was present at the most important exhibitions and De Koninck himself designed brochures showing the CUBEX system in meticulously designed axonometrics (Ruëgg 1989) (Figure 3). The commercial success of the system was undisputed, resulting in the fact that the CUBEX kitchen provided one of the very few instances where modernist design indeed was able to achieve the social objectives it aimed for (Vandenbreeden and Vanlaethem 1996).

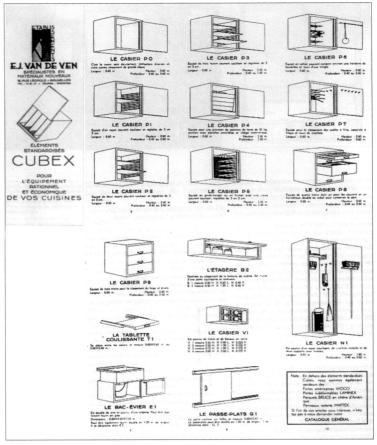

Figure 3
List of standardized CUBEX elements from a brochure published by the Van de Ven company, about 1935 (Ruëgg 1989). Courtesy Archive d'Architecture Moderne, Brussels.

The 1930s also saw the arrival of electric appliances (Figure 4). Electricity was considered a "miracle drug" that would transform the kitchen into a place of extreme tidiness and elegance and would tremendously relieve the housewife's work. Gilles wrote:

> Thanks to it (the electrified kitchen), the asphyxiation in the kitchen that resembled a smoke-filled slum in the age of coal, will disappear. No longer is the housewife obliged to get up before dawn to light the moody stove, depending on favourable or unfavourable breezes, on the draught of the chimney, on the wood being either dry or humid, on untraceable matches, . . . The electrified kitchen makes itself felt as an admirable result of tidiness and elegance (Gilles 1931: 889).[22]

Dust and ashes would be things of the past as soon as the electric stove conquered the kitchen.

In addition, although to a smaller degree, the use of gas in the kitchen was also recommended. The gas cooker, like the electric one, would make the kitchen more tidy and hygienic. As well as the cooker, the refrigerator—powered by electricity as well as gas—was greatly promoted. It was considered an essential apparatus in a modern kitchen: "because it makes possible to conserve and use all the food in stead of having to throw it away, as is so often the case in summer" (X 1932c: 32).[23] The refrigerator would facilitate the work of the housewife since the food no longer had to be stored in the cellar—the coolest place in the home "which obliged the mistress of the home to cover, each day, numerous tiring displacements that were often even difficult and dangerous" (X 1939g: 324).[24] One mainly recommended built-in refrigerators, because they could be completely integrated into the kitchen equipment and were cheaper, since they had to be covered at only one side (X 1932c; Figure 5).

Figure 4
Examples of electric kitchen apparatus (from top to bottom): a potato peeler; a machine to grind meat, coffee, etc.; a mixer; a bread slicer (Gilles 1931).

MACHINES POUR CUISINES MODERNES

Figure 5
Example of a kitchen equipped with a built-in refrigerator (Frielux) (X 1932c).

The Belgian housewife occupied an important—be it rather passive—place in the architectural discourse regarding the rationalization of the kitchen. (There are no indications of close collaborations between architects and housewives or housewives' associations, as existed in the Netherlands or Germany.) The arrangement and equipment of the kitchen had to be optimally tuned to "female labor" in order for her to work as efficiently as possible. To fully enjoy all the advantages the rational kitchen could offer, the woman herself was supposed to put in effort too: she ought to have a thorough domestic knowledge. For this an appropriate domestic education was necessary, otherwise, the efforts of the architects to design functional kitchens could prove useless, as De Koninck puts it:

> the modern architects stress unanimously that, without an appropriate education [for the housewives], their efforts to realize a better use of the rooms and materials and finally to obtain a maximum of comfort in the house could remain sterile (De Koninck 1931: 105-6).[25]

Gilles stresses moreover that the rational kitchen would free the educated housewife from domestic drudgery:

> The housewives are no longer slaves . . . In the bright rooms, with mechanized cupboards, with neat and precise equipment one next to the other, the work is finally synchronised. And harmony rules! Less exhausted, freeer, better prepared the housewife, works without rancour. Through organization, through planning, overstrain, irritability, even neurosis, are banished out of the home (Gilles 1936: 563).[26]

Working would be pleasant, hygienic, and comfortable in the modern kitchen: "As pride and joy of the good mistress of the home, as well as of the servant, the modern kitchen, neat, elegant, is an assurance of a good temper and a continual source of economy" (X 1935b).[27]

It is fairly typical that Gilles presents the rational kitchen as applicable to every home, regardless of class or income considerations. Although Belgian society at that time was socially stratified and ideologically "pillarized,"[28] Belgian architects were of the opinion that the rational kitchen had to be universal and affordable for everybody. Architects had to make an effort to offer everyone an efficient and healthy kitchen:

> Served by their natural methodical intellect and sense of order, the modern architects should rapidly fix the principles of the practical organisation of the kitchen, whether it concerns the kitchen of the poor or the kitchen of the rich. Both should be economical, hygienic and comfortable (Gilles 1931: 888).[29]

Social reality, however, proved to be not completely in tune with the architects' presuppositions. Their ideas concerning the rational kitchen were not met with the same enthusiasm across the social strata, as can be gathered from a study of women's magazines directed at different social groups.

THE RATIONAL KITCHEN IN WOMEN'S MAGAZINES

Clearly the attitudes of the different women's magazines vis-à-vis the issue of the rational kitchen differed considerably. Women's magazines meant for bourgeois and middle-class women paid great attention to the rational kitchen; women's magazines intended for working-class women or farmer's wives, on the other hand, dealt mainly with the "living-kitchen" and only rarely mentioned the efficient "work-kitchen."

The bourgeois and middle-class magazines treated the rational kitchen as a way to facilitate domestic tasks—aggravated mainly because of the servant crisis.[30] Among them, the most outspoken feminist journal considered the rational kitchen essential in the struggle for emancipation: if the housekeeping would be less time- and effort-consuming, women could spend more time on intellectual self-development and, if she wanted, accede to the labor market. In 1933, Made Droesbeke Cocq stated in *Egalité*—the organ of the Groupement belge pour l'Affranchissement de la Femme (Belgian Grouping for the Emancipation of the Woman)[31]—that the kitchen was the basis of the household, because from this room the vital functions spread out across the house (Droesbeke Cocq 1935). While in earlier days the kitchen had been a large and charming family room, the circumstances in 1933, she argued, when land was more and more scarce and time became increasingly precious, necessitated rationalization of the kitchen because the domestic activity had to be done rapidly and with minimal effort. In accordance with architectural discourse, she stated that the modern kitchen had to be small, organized, and equipped in a rational and logical way—like a laboratory—and conceived for domestic work only, because living was out of place in a kitchen.

In 1934 the Secrétariat des Oeuvres Sociales de la Fédération Nationale des Femmes Libérales (Secretariat for Social Works of the National Federation of Liberal Women) organized two conferences on household rationalization, aimed at liberating women from the drudgery of domestic slavery. One of the speakers was the architect Claire-Lucille Henrotin, who discussed the "rational equipment of a kitchen and washhouse." The report of this lecture in *Egalité* shows the circulation-plan of a rational kitchen discussed earlier (S. S. 1934a, b).

Other women's magazines meant for bourgeois and middle-class women, such as *Modeblad/Rijk der Vrouw*, *Chez Soi* or *Femmes d'aujourd'hui*, also promoted rationalization of the household and the kitchen as an answer to the servant crisis. Often, the principles and characteristics of the rational kitchen, as dealt with in architectural discourse were presented within the pages of such magazines. An illustration in one of the articles shows the fully equipped CUBEX kitchen (Guerin 1937a).

An annoyance for the authors of those magazines was, apparently, that too many women did not recognize the importance of the kitchen when looking for a new home.

> Everything is nice, exactly as one already searched for a long time, but the kitchen . . . there's fair amount of wrong with it! Not only the young inexperienced women pay too little attention to construction and arrangement of the kitchen, the more experienced housewives too take notice of the kitchen only in the last resort (X 1935a).[32]

as one can read in an article dated 1937. The kitchen deserved nonetheless a great deal of attention, since:

> It's yet round the kitchen that the entire domestic life turns, and, to the extent that this room is well arranged or badly, it will be pleasant or sad and somber to occupy, it's there where the meals are prepared: and don't forget that it is on those that depends a great deal of your good or bad mood (Guerin 1937a: 16).[33]

The author of this article fulminated against the "basement kitchen," that was humid, badly lit and ventilated, and caused additional exhaustion because of the extra walking up and down stairs: "For all I care, if circumstances require that I am obliged to occupy a house with a basement-kitchen, I would rather sacrifice a salon than accepting that my culinary laboratory is put in the ground!" (Guerin 1937a, 16).[34]

Furthermore, those magazines gave their members a lot of tips on how to achieve a fairly cheap and practically equipped kitchen: a dish rack above the plate rack of the sink so that the dishes could dry by themselves (X 1934a), a table with wheels for the clean dishes to be brought to the cupboard all at once (Guerin 1937b: 19), the use of a stool in order to work with less effort (Guerin 1937b: 26), chairs with drawers, and a long bin on the inside of the door for extra storage (X 1937a). In addition, it was pointed out that a rational position-ing of the furniture and efficient working methods in the kitchen could result in considerable saving of space, time, and effort (Guerin 1937b; Nicht Boub 1926). This well-meant advice gives rise to the suspicion that the kitchens of most readers of those magazines were still a mishmash of purchased and self-made furniture. Hence one can conclude that the fully standardized and built-in kitchen, promoted by architectural discourse, had not yet found actual application in most middle-class and bourgeois families.

A specific case is that of the magazine *La femme Belge,* the periodical of Angéline Japsenne's organization, which we encountered in the Introduction of this article.[35] This magazine took the issue of the rational kitchen to be an important one, not so much for the sake of its own readership, however, but mostly for the working classes they were supposed to be dealing with in their charity work. Catholic bourgeois women who were interested in women and social issues and who struggled against the slums and bad living conditions in workmen's houses, thus paid a lot of attention to the functional minimum dwelling and to the modern comfort that accompanied it, such as a rational kitchen (Japsenne 1929, 1930). In the article mentioned earlier, Japsenne eagerly defended the idea that one had to live in the living room and that the kitchen was to be a separate room, solely destined for domestic activities (Japsenne 1930). The discourse of those catholic women stated that the aim was to help the housewife to perfect her housekeeping, so that she would have more time left to spend with her husband and children. Clearly, in the opinion of this group, the natural place of a mother was at home and her primary task in life was to take care of husband and children (De Weerdt 1980; Japsenne 1931).

Strangely enough, the women's magazines addressed to working-class women themselves, (*Vrouwenbeweging, La Ligue des Femmes, Stem der Vrouw, La Famille Prévoyante*), did not share this fascination for the rational kitchen. The plea made by catholic bourgeois women for rational kitchens in workmen's homes, did apparently not make it to the women of lower classes themselves. The periodical of the Nationaal Verbond van Christelijke Vrouwengilden (National League of Christian Women's Guilds)[36] for example, opted for a living-kitchen for practical reasons (financial restrictions) as well as ideological ones (inten-sifying family life). Since an average working-class family could afford only one stove and no cooker,[37] out of necessity cooking, domestic activities, and family life usually happened in one and the same room. A kitchen conceived as a small separate room would thus inevitably degenerate into a messy and busy room where one could not possibly organize family life (X 1939a, f). It was argued that, due to shift systems, meetings, and other activities outside the house, the ties between the family members had already slackened. The Christelijke Vrouwengilden therefore, who considered, just like other catholic organizations, motherhood, marriage, and housekeeping to be the natural vocations of a woman, thought that it was of vital importance that the woman managed to make the few occasions the family came together as pleasant as possible, in order to make sure that husband and children would stay attached to their home (X 1933). A large living-kitchen where the family could, in perfect harmony, eat together, work together, live together, relax together . . . was thus considered essential to secure family stability. Or, as one put it in 1939 with regard to "mother's kitchen" (Figure 6)

> Not only because everything is spick and span, not only because mother takes care of a good fire, not only because we find food there, but also because there we meet one another . . . oh, I can't really tell why: we are at home there—and that's all! (X 1939a).[38]

The living-kitchen not only had to be large but also needed to be arranged and equipped in a sensible way. For solving this "puzzle" the housewife was held responsible (X 1939a). To this end, she was offered numerous tips. The peri-odicals published examples of well-equipped living-kitchens (X 1929a, 1932b), showed solutions to facilitate the combination of various activities—e.g. railings

Figure 6
An example of a large living-kitchen (Sint-Niklaas), such as every working-class family should have (according to *Vrouwenbeweging*) (X 1939f).

round the stove so that little children would not get burned (X 1938b), a table that could be pulled out during meals (X 1938c). Simplicity and uniformity in the arrangement of the living-kitchen were considered important (Martha 1938; X 1938b). Tips were given to organize the household in a more rational (and thus less exhausting) way: a rolling serving table (X 1939b), suggestions about good lighting (B. J. 1937, 1939; V. M. 1938; X 1929b; X 1938a), advice with regard to a good working position (X 1932d), efficient furniture that could be made by the husband (B. J. 1933, 1937), the use of a stool while working (B. J. 1939), a haybox (V. M. 1938). It was not until 1938 that electric and gas cookers appeared in the pages of *Vrouwenbeweging* (V. M. 1938).

At the end of the 1930s the Christelijke Vrouwengilden began to put up a real fight for "family kitchens" (X 1939a, c). In 1939 *Vrouwenbeweging* published a "good example" of a plan for a working-class house, designed by Angéline Japsenne (X 1939e; Figure 7). Whereas she had earlier spoken out in favor of the work-kitchen (Japsenne 1929), she now took an opposite view, urged, no doubt, by the realization that the Depression years had not brought the wealth needed to afford the more "rational" solution. A basic requirement to her was the request for space: the family needed enough space to be able to live in an appropriate way. In particular, the familial kitchen had to be large enough.

If the catholic working-class organizations opted for a family kitchen, the catholic Boerinnenbond (Farmers' Wives Association),[39] hardly paid any atten-tion to the kitchen question during the interwar period. In *De Boerin,* the terms "kitchen" and "living room" were almost interchangeable and both referred to one room where one cooked as well as lived. Apparently, the living-kitchen was a self-evident reality for this rural group. Whenever the magazine did pay atten-tion to issues of interior design, it was to advocate the qualities of order, hy-giene and simplicity. Kitchen cupboards, for example, with curls, tips, and columns were strongly advised against, because that was asking for extra work. Only two possibilities were considered appropriate: one could opt for built-in cupboards that occupied little space and could be made with little money, or one could choose a large, comfortable, simple and solid cupboard (Matant 1928; Figure 8). Order and neatness were essential to make the house more pleas-ant, according to the principles: "a place for everything and everything in its place," "a time for everything and everything on time," and "purity and tidiness everywhere" (M. L. 1920). This magazine also gave a number of tips: a good

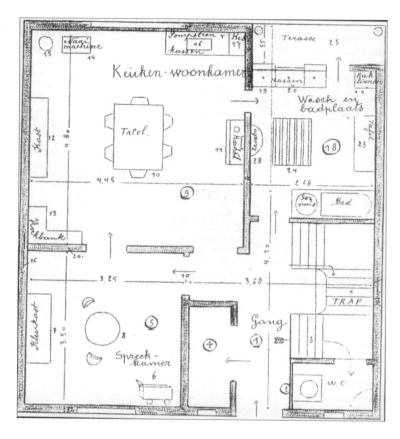

Figure 7
Plan for a working-class
house, designed by
A. Japsenne (X 1939e).

Figure 8
On the left, an example of a
"bad" kitchen cupboard (too
many curls, tips, etc.). On the
right, an example of a "good"
kitchen cupboad (large,
simple, comfortable, solid)
(according to *De Boerin*)
(Matant 1928).

working position, the use of equipment, organizing and planning the work in an efficient manner, assigning a fixed place for all utensils (J. W. 1935; X 1934b).

Whereas the catholic periodicals favored the idea of the woman as housewife and homemaker, their socialist counterparts fostered the ideal of a combination of marriage, motherhood, and paid employment.[40] If they paid little attention to the rational kitchen, this neglect was not grounded on an ideological basis. Caring for husband and children was also from a socialist point of view one of the main tasks for a woman. Nevertheless, the Socialistische Vrouwenbeweging also saw women's work outside the home as the key to economic emancipation. Moreover, many working-class families did not cope financially if the woman stayed at home. A woman therefore had to be free to choose whether or not she took on a job (De Weerdt 1997).

In the early 1920s, the Socialistische Vrouwenbeweging had insisted on the implementation of collective services, such as communal laundries and kitchens. However, those services were slow in materializing. Therefore, the socialist women's magazines also took up the issue of rational housekeeping, giving numerous tips to facilitate domestic tasks, for example, on using a self-heater or haybox (X 1927), on the application of electricity (such as the electric cooker) (Heyman 1935), on the importance of a good lighting and how to achieve it (X 1932a), on rational furniture (X 1937b).

The rational kitchen as promoted in architects' discourse, however, received only sporadic attention. Probably because they considered the well-equipped work-kitchen unaffordable, socialist women opted instead for a large and airy living-kitchen, where each member of the family could be busy without disturbing the others (X 1936). Austerity and efficiency, simplicity and reliability had to dominate in the arrangement of the living-kitchen, to make it a true home, a peaceful island in a busy society (Rombaut 1924; X 1936). On the rare occasion that a rational kitchen was shown and discussed, as in the case of the kitchen designed by a Swedish institute and presented in *La Famille Prévoyante* in 1936, it was treated as something almost futuristic (X 1937b).

If the architects' magazines were not mentioning any close collaboration between architects and domestic experts, neither did the women's magazines, although they regularly appealed to the architects to consult women for the design of houses and kitchens (Japsenne 1930; X 1932a, 1939d, f). In addition, women were advised to interrogate architects about their experiences with regard to the rational kitchen (Bourguet 1934; Helin and Hubeaux 1936). But, apparently, those appeals did not generate solid, well-documented cooperation during the interwar period in Belgium.

BUILT REALITY

As can already be glimpsed from the reception of the kitchen question in women's magazines, the universality that was presupposed in the architects' discussion of the rational kitchen did not fully materialize in the built reality of newly constructed houses and apartments. Whereas the rational kitchen did make its way into the bourgeois and middle-class homes of the 1930s, most of the workmen's houses built in the interwar period had to do without a functional kitchen.

In fact by the time that modernist architects had developed the basic models for the minimum standard dwelling, they were no longer called upon to design social housing in Belgium. Whereas the country had produced exemplary modern housing in the early 1920s, with famous neighborhoods such as Logis-Floréal and Kapelleveld, from 1925 onwards the more radically modern architects were excluded from the domain of social housing. This reorientation basically had to do with a shift in the political power balance (De Meulder 1999; Smets 1977). The socialists, who had participated in the government right after the First World War, were excluded from it after 1926, when catholics and liberals dominated Belgian politics again. With the disappearance of a socialist housing policy, the modernist models were no longer accepted. The better-off classes feared the modernist neighborhoods, which they considered "red bulwarks," they were skeptical about the state initiative promoted by socialists, turned down collective housing and promoted the individual house and private property. In addition, since the middle of the 1920s, resistance to the modernist movement as a whole increased, because it was associated with revolutionary strategies and because the houses designed by the modernists were considered too cold, too sober, and too functional to appeal to the wider public.

All this resulted in the fact that the working-class housing that got built in Belgium after 1925 did not apply the modernist principles—among them the rational kitchen—but fell back on older models. This was supported by authors such as A. Puissant, who argued in 1931 that the minimum dwelling, equipped with a rational kitchen, was not yet appropriate for this type of housing because the necessary facilities to realize this hygienic and comfortable "functional habitat"—such as sewerage, potable water supply, and gas pipes—were often not available in the locations meant for working-class housing. Moreover, he argued, appliances such as refrigerators were too expensive for workmen's budgets (Puissant 1931).

Whereas the modernists' viewpoint was thus well articulated and clearly present in many architectural publications, it did not really dominate the actual field of building. A lot of architects felt they had to formulate less "radical" solutions for the miserable living conditions of the working-class.[41] Instead of replacing the current type-plan by a completely new and modern one, they just tried to modify the existing one to provide somewhat more comfort and living quality in the workmen's houses. There was, however, no unanimity as to the question of the separate work-kitchen versus the living-kitchen. At the national level, the authorities of the national housing society preferred a distinction between domestic activities and family life: a large living room and a small kitchen–washhouse; a lot of the local housing societies on the other hand wanted a large kitchen–washhouse and a small salon (presumably only used for special occasions) (Puissant 1931: 8). Puissant himself agreed with the second group and considered a large living-kitchen, where domestic activities and family life were harmoniously combined, as the more desirable option. The type-plans for workmen's homes thus hardly changed during the interwar period. It was not until after the second World War that the modernist functional plan—provided with a rational kitchen—made its entry in Belgian social housing.[42]

In marked contrast with workers' housing, dwelling forms for the middle classes did change rather profoundly. From 1925 onwards, the apartment made its entrance in Belgium as a new way of living for the bourgeoisie (Hennaut 1996). Considering the sharply rising construction and land prices, the cost-sharing possibility of an apartment made this way of living attractive. Moreover, living at only one level simplified the domestic tasks, which created the possibility of reducing the amount of domestic servants. It was in these bourgeois apartments that modern comfort—promoted by the modernists—first appeared in any significant quantity. The rationally equipped kitchen, central heating, electrification, etc. were indispensable elements for this modern way of bourgeois living.

Rationalization thus was considered important for the design, organization, and equipment of an apartment. According to Victor Rogister the objective when designing an apartment, was to achieve a rational, time- and effort-saving plan by means of a profound study of the domestic activity and the relationships between the different rooms (Rogister 1935). The kitchen had to be located adjacent to the dining room. Moreover, the kitchen should be rationally organized and well-equipped. Jean-F. Collin states it in 1936 as follows:

> The primitive kitchen of our grandmothers has evolved to the point in time of becoming a real laboratory: built-in cupboards, refrigerators, kitchen sink equipped with hot and cold water, gas or electric cooker, soap dish, matches holder, dustbin, etc., constitute from now on the typical suite of furniture in this useful room (Collin 1936: 503).[43]

In 1946, Jean Delhaye published a small manual: *L'appartement d'aujourd'hui* (Delhaye 1946), a book that can be considered a summary of the practice of designing apartments in the interwar period. He described in detail the distribution and equipment of three apartment types: "minimum apartments" for rather modest incomes, "average apartments" for those with more money, and "very spacious and luxurious apartments" for the very rich (Figure 9). Not surprisingly, Delhaye considered the kitchen to be the most important room for domestic activity and that it had to be equipped and arranged in a rational and efficient way (Figure 10). With regard to the size of the kitchen, he stated:

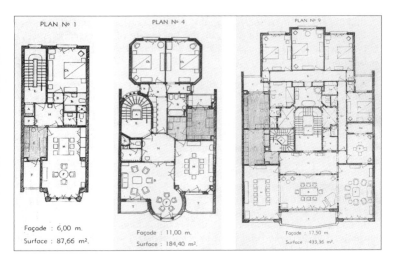

Figure 9
From left to right: an example of a "minimum apartment," an "average apartment," and a "luxury apartment" (Delhaye 1946).

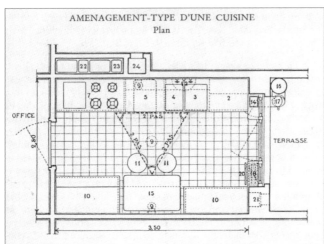

Figure 10
Type-plan of a rational kitchen in an apartment (according to Delhaye 1946).

Dans une cuisine, la plus grande fréquence des déplacements se fait entre l'évier, la cuisinière et la table. Rechercher à séparer ces trois éléments de l'équipement par des équidistances minima constitue l'un des objectifs essentiels à atteindre.

Légende :

1. Armoires évier
2. Tablette évier
3. Grande cuvette
4. Cuvette de rinçage
5. Egouttoir
6. Table desserte
7. Cuisinière
8. Casiers
9. Luminaires
10. Armoires
11. Tabourets
12. Robinets mélangeur
13. Dosseret
14. Boîte à ordures
15. Table
16. Tube vide-poubelles
17. Evacuor-vidoir
18. Radiateur
19. Hotte
20. Porte-essuie
21. Ventilation armoire
22. Conduit fumée
23. Conduit ventilation
24. Gaine canalisations

the kitchen should be sufficiently large in order to contain easily all the equipment and to allow an easy circulation, and sufficiently small in order to prevent that the kitchen is used as dining room. The utilization of the kitchen for taking meals is a very bad habit that, unfortunately!, is profoundly anchored in Belgium (Delhaye 1946: 113).[44]

Furthermore, according to Delhaye a good husband—or *pater familias*—would never buy or rent an apartment without paying a lot of attention to the kitchen:

By the acquisition of an apartment, the good family father sees to it that the kitchen is perfect, or capable of becoming it by means of transformations. Like this, he assures the housewife of the facilities she has the right on, and, indirectly, one shall reap several advantages (Delhaye 1946: 111).[45]

A few examples demonstrate that the rational kitchen had been quite generally adopted in bourgeois milieus. The first is the Résidence Léopold in Brussels, designed in 1937 by R. Verwilghen and J.J. Eggerickx. All sixty-two apartments of this block were equipped with CUBEX kitchens (X 1938d). The same kitchens were installed in the Résidence Plissart, a block of apartments in Brussels created by the architect Stanislas Jasinski in the second half of the 1930s (Jasinski 1939). Architect Sylvain de Praetere also provided rational kitchens—though not CUBEX this time—in an apartment building in Anderlecht. These kitchens were considered remarkable for several reasons: the complete tiling, the built-in cupboards, the sink, the automatic chute, the electric cooker and built-in refrigerator (Deletang 1937).

In addition to the apartment, urban or suburban individual homes also underwent a transformation during the interwar period. The large and prestigious bourgeois houses from the nineteenth century were far too expensive and required too many servants.

More and more, the needs of this age impose us with regard to the bourgeois house "the one made's home" [sic], where the service can be guaranteed by one maid only. This brings along an increasingly large simplification of the home (De Ridder 1925: 403).[46]

as one put it in *La Technique des Travaux* in 1925. Thus one had to study and rethink the organization of the plan of the home, in order to facilitate household work. The principles of household rationalization would be very useful to this end; the objective was to arrive at a rational house. According to Victor Duykers (in 1933), in earlier times too much attention was given to decoration, to the detriment of the plan that, by consequence, was not practical enough, and the domestic equipment, which was almost completely neglected. Duykers stated that being very functional, the small bourgeois home—or the middle-class home—answered to the program of a rational house (Duykers 1933: 414).

Obviously, these rational houses had to be provided with a rational kitchen, the preeminent place to adopt scientific household principles. In particular, the small bourgeois home was inextricably bound up with the efficient kitchen. De Koninck, for example, designed in 1930 in Oudergem a small bourgeoisie home with a rational kitchen. The kitchen was fully equipped: a wall of CUBEX cupboards with hatch, a sink combined with a large granite table, a gas cooker and a cooker hood (De Koninck 1930; Figure 11). Two years later, De Koninck created, in the same suburb, another middle-class house equipped with a functional CUBEX kitchen (Flouquet 1933). The dimensions of this kitchen were determined by the equipment and by the demands of the household work. Here too, a cupboard-wall accessible from both sides separated the kitchen from the dining room. In Antwerp, Rik Jacops used a rational kitchen in a functional habitation. The kitchen was a real laboratory for the housewife, where one could work easily, comfortably, and hygienically (Deletang 1936; Figure 12). As a final example, a rational equipped kitchen in a habitation in Brussels (Ukkel) was designed by Raphaël Delville (Flouquet 1936; Figure 13).

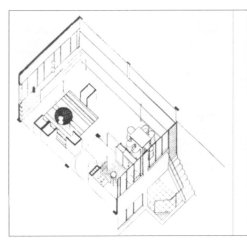

Figure 11
The small bourgeois house at Oudergem designed by L.-H. De Koninck, 1930. On the left, perspective of the house; the kitchen is located in the lower left corner. On the right, a view of the kitchen fully equipped with CUBEX cupboards (De Koninck 1930).

Figure 12
The "functional" habitation at Antwerp from Rik Jacops. Plans of the ground floor, first, and second floors. The kitchen is situated on the first level (the gray-colored zone on the right) (Deletang 1936).

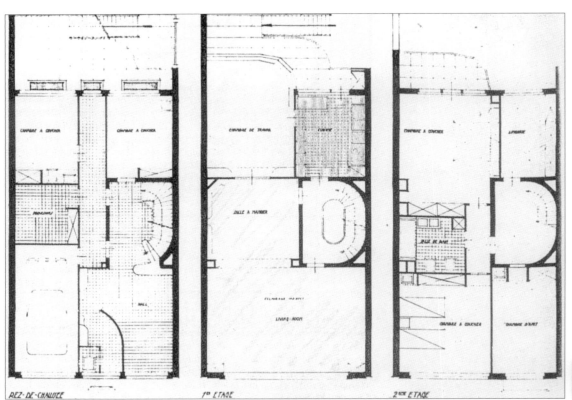

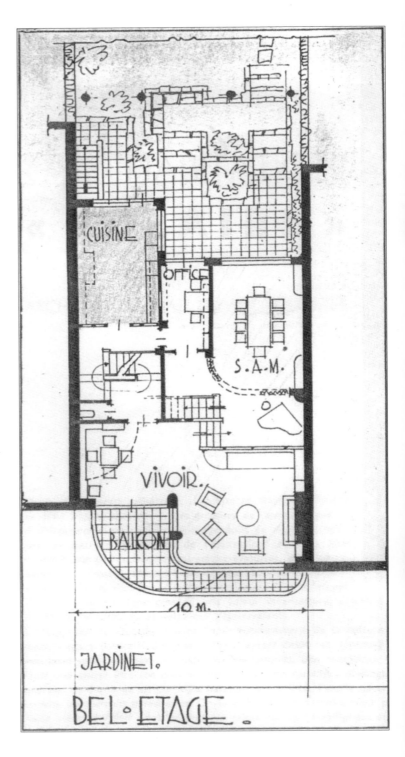

Figure 13
Plan of the habitation
designed by R. Delville in
Brussels (Flouquet 1936).

CONCLUSION

It thus seems that Belgian modernist architects were very knowledgeable about the rationalization of the household and did apply rational kitchens whenever they saw the opportunity. The public in general, however, was far from convinced that such a kitchen provided the best solution to their needs. Whereas both kitchen and bathroom were firmly established figures in architects' discourse, it was not until the postwar years that they were readily accepted as models to be followed across the whole range of social strata. What we now see as clearly identifiable kitchen or bathroom appliances were in fact migrating through different rooms in workmen's housing from the interwar period in Belgium. Next to the architects' logic, which differentiated between activities related to the processing of food—which should be concentrated in the kitchen—and activities related to the cleansing of the body—for which the bathroom was the correct venue—there was an alternative logic operating. (Figure 7)

This alternative logic was not based upon the different realms associated with the needs to feed or to clean the body, but rather with the kind of provision that was necessary to answer different needs. It arranged separately everything to do with fire and heat from everything to do with water. Within this logic, it was fairly evident to have a large living-kitchen where one source of heat provided both the energy for cooking as well as the warmth needed for a range of other activities—sitting together, knitting, doing homework, reading the newspaper, playing games, etc. All the activities relying upon the availability of water were referred to another room—the washhouse—where the dishes were done, but also personal cleaning rituals were carried out. Thus one finds in some schemes the by now awkward combination of a bathtub next to a sink for the dishes. This positioning of bathtub or shower was also motivated by a concern that washing needed to be done when coming in filthy after a day of hard (rural) work, rather than in the morning in order to get ready to work—which is a custom more related to urban living conditions.

In all probability there was also another reason why the rational work-kitchen was not accepted for working-class housing. This reason is associated with assumptions about privacy and propriety. In the eyes of many architects, working-class families were wrong in concentrating all activities in the kitchen, when they also had another, better room available (Henrotin 1932a). For the people involved, however, it seems to have been very important to have one "proper" place, called the "nice room" or the "best place," in which to receive higher ranked visitors, such as the priest or the doctor (relatives, friends, and neighbors would be welcomed in the kitchen instead). This room, usually the front room, was to show off nice furniture and valued possessions. Having a large kitchen where all disturbing activities took place allowed housewives to keep the nice room at all times clean and tidy, and they took great pride in this.[47] Sacrificing the best room for a family room cum rational kitchen was, from their point of view, not at all an attractive idea.

For the middle classes and the bourgeoisie, on the other hand, applying the rational kitchen did not disrupt the customary boundaries between the different parts of the house, since the kitchen was previously the domain of the servants and thus had never functioned as a family room. Clearly modernist ideas regarding the rational kitchen were much more in tune with the needs and expectations of the higher classes of the population. This of course is hardly surprising given the fact that, after all, architects themselves usually belonged to the middle or upper class.

NOTES

1. This article is the partial result of two research projects funded by the Fund for Scientific Research Flanders (FWO): "Developing a scientific model of everyday dwelling, from the perspective of architectural theory" (promoters Hilde Heynen and André Loeckx, 2001–2004) and "His work, her house. Investigation of the social mediation of architectural ideas on dwelling in Flanders 1920–1970" (promoters Leen Van Molle, Hilde Heynen, Veerle Draulans and Patrick Pasture, 2003–2006).

2. In 1928, modernist architects—who had been able to get in touch thanks to avant-garde press and exhibitions—organized themselves at an international level in the CIAM group. This international group stood up for modern architecture. Architecture became associated with economic and political issues, one strove for a new and classless society. At stake was a homogenous society with universal needs. Serial production and standardization were deemed necessary to achieve this goal (Van der Woud 1983).

3. The intention the members of the CIAM group had with the "Wohnung für das Existenzminimum" (Minimum Habitat) was to create a universal house, identical and affordable for everyone; a house that would express a classless society. By means of scientific analysis, the "biological minimum requirements" of a person, and resulting from this the dimensions of the house, were determined. In addition, the house was studied from the point of view of a person as a human being that needs air, light, warmth and rest. Moreover, the Minimum Habitat would formulate an answer to the exhaustion of the housewife—resulting from the exertion of domestic tasks—by means of good organization and arrangement of the house, and a rational kitchen as a main requirement. Rationalization and standardization were the key issues in making all the foregoing possible (Bourgeois 1930).

4. English translation of: "des locaux de jour, de nuit et de service, agencé pour être facilement entretenus et agréablement habités; une petite cuisine, mais si pratiquement disposée que les plus vulgaires besognes s'y feront proprement, . . ." (Japsenne 1929: 534).

5. English translation of: "Il réalisait, en effet, un effort considérable vers la solution d'un problème toujours angoissant chez nous: la conquête, par la classe ouvrière, de logements attrayantes, sains, munis de tout le confort amené par les progrès actuels de la science appliquée" (Japsenne 1930: 580).

6. English translation of: "Il s'agit d'abord d'aménager une cuisine, où les travaux ménagers puissent s'accomplir d'une façon hygiénique, amenant une fatigue normale de la femme ménagère, mais non un émuissement que leur nature ne justifie pas" (Japsenne 1930: 582).

7. English translation of: "Mais de grâce, Messieurs les architectes, consultez des femmes de ménages avant de faire vos plans!" (Japsenne 1930: 583).

8. Around the turn of the century, the American engineer F. W. Taylor (1865–1915) developed "scientific management" for increasing the productive capacity of factory workers. The "Taylorism" or efficiency theory involved an accurate investigation of every task by means of time and motion studies, with the intention of rationalizing and standardizing this task so that one could obtain a good result with as little effort as possible. At the beginning of the twentieth century, Christine Frederick applied the principles of Taylorism to housekeeping, giving the movement the rationalization of the household—founded by Catherine Beecher in the nineteenth century—a new impetus (Beer 1994; Wilke 1998).

9. Margarete Schutte-Lihotzky (1897–2000), Viennese by birth, was a socialist activist and devoted her professional life to the improvement of the living conditions of the working class. In 1921, she worked as an architect for the Viennese Siedlungen movement. In the middle of the 1920s, the German architect Ernst May got her to Frankfurt-am-Main where she designed, amongst other things, the Frankfurter Küche (Geist and Krausse 1984; Henderson 1996).

10. Research for this article was conducted in the archive of architect Huib Hoste (at the university archive of the Katholieke Universiteit Leuven) and the archive of architect-urbanist Raphaël Verwilghen (at the Instituut voor Stedenbouw en Ruimtelijke Ordening, Katholieke Universiteit Leuven). The architectural magazines used for this investigation are: Bâtir, L'Habitation à Bon Marché, La Technique des Travaux, La Cité/Tekhné, and Opbouwen. Consulted women magazines were: La femme Belge, Egalité, Chez Soi, and Femmes d'aujourd'hui. The investigation was facilitated by previous

student work excerpting this and other material, under the guidance of Leen Van Molle (women's magazines) and Luc Verpoest (architectural magazines).

11. Victor Bourgeois and Huib Hoste were present at the first CIAM congress—CIAMI—in 1928 at La Sarraz. At the second CIAM congress—CIAM II—the Belgian delegation was more extensive, amongst others Victor Bourgeois, Louis-Herman De Koninck, J. J. Eggerickx, and Raphaël Verwilghen attended the congress. Further, CIAM III took place in Belgium, more specifically in Brussels in 1930.

12. English translation of: "*La cuisine est la pièce du logis dont l'équipement mérite d'être étudié avec le plus de précision. Ne s'agit-il pas de créer le cadre pratique ou la ménagère passera une importe partie de ses jours; au détriment de sa santé si le problème est mal résolu*" (Gaspard 1933: 146).

13. English translation of: "*. . . agencer une cuisine rationnellement, le but le plus important étant atteint: travail ménager facilité, réduction de fatigues, accroissement de santé et augmentation de bien-être pour la ménagère*" (De Koninck 1933: 736).

14. At this, apparently, there was no real unanimity: De Koninck, for example, distinguished two activity centers—"preparing of the meals" and "using and maintaining of the kitchenware" whereas Pierre Gilles discerned five activity groups—"putting ready the requirements," "cooking," "cleaning the objects and foods," "serving," and "preserving the food," and Claire-Lucille Henrotin divided the activities in three groups—"preparing the meals," "putting away and cleaning up the material after the supper," and "doing the dishes."

15. Henrotin 1933: 9–10; she had already designed this plan in 1930, as one can derive from a document from the archive of Huib Hoste that shows this plan accompanied by the following text: "Equipment of a kitchen in a minimum habitat—circulation—Claire Henrotin—La Louvière 1930" (English translation).

16. English translation of: "*. . . Prévoyant à coté de la salle commune, une petite cuisinée où la ménagère a sous la main, rangé suivant un plan étudié, tout ce qui est nécessaire à la préparation des repas. La cuisine ainsi conçue peut seule mériter le titre de cuisine rationnelle*" (Henrotin 1932: 25).

17. English translation of: "*Het treft ons allereerst hoe men tegenwoordig niet meer van keukeninrichting, doch van keukenuitrusting gewaagt. Men kan zeggen dat de inrichting bestaat in de juiste opstelling van gootsteen en kooktoestel. Dit is echter ondoelmatig gebleken indien de huisvrouw naast gootsteen en kachel de aldaar nodige huisraad niet vlak bij de hand heeft. Zo is men er toe gekomen de keuken uit te rusten met de nodige vaste kasten die telkens opgevat en geschikt zijn voor hetgene zijzy moeten bergen*" (Hoste 1937: 77).

18. English translation of: "*Si la première condition à remplir par le local servant de cuisine est de permettre une disposition logique du mobilier, celui-ci à son tour, pour être rationnel, doit faciliter et rendre pour ainsi dire automatique le rangement raisonné de tout l'outillage nécessité par les divers travaux culinaires*" (Henrotin 1932c: 51).

19. English translation of: "*. . . s'il fallait fabriquer pour chaque cas particulier des meubles spéciaux, les pris de revient à l'unité seraient nécessairement très élevés et il faut ainsi arriver à une fabrication en série en standardisant*" (Henrotin 1932c: 51).

20. English translation of: "*Malgré la qualité et le nombre important de logements, j'estime que le manqué de l'universalité de la conception ne résoud qu'imparfaitment le problème. Chaque cuisine, composée de 3 ou 4 éléments seulement, oblige les architectes à n'adopter qu'un nombre limité de modèles d'agencement*" L. H. De Koninck, quoted in Delevoy et al. 1980: 88.

21. Van de Ven was an industrialist who first came onto the Belgian market in 1920 with the import of standardized doors of the mark "Woco." It was a great success and Van de Ven brought the fabrication over to Belgium where

he also started to produce sash windows. At this, J. J Eggericx was enlisted as consultant, through which at once the contact between CIAMB and Van de Ven was made (Ruëgg 1989: 208–9).

22. English translation of: *"Grâce à elle, finie l'asphyxie dans le taudis enfumé qu'était la cuisine à l'âge du charbon, quand il fallait se lever à l'aube pour allumer un fourneau fantaisiste, dépendant des vents favorables ou non, du tirage de la chéminéé, du bois sec ou humide, des allumettes introuvable, etc . . . La cuisine électrique s'impose comme un admirable resultat de propreté et d'élégance"* (Gilles 1931: 889).

23. English translation of: *"économie à réaliser sur tous les aliments que l'on pourrait conserver et utiliser au lieu de devoir le jeter, comme c'est si souvent le cas en été"* (X 1932c: 32).

24. English translation of: *". . . la maîtresse de maison s'impose, chaque jour, de nombreux déplacements fatigants et souvent même pénibles, voire dangereux"* (X 1939g: 324).

25. English translation of: *". . . les architectes modernes sont unanimes à affirmer que, sans l'éducation scolaire appropriée, leurs efforts pour une meilleure utilisation des locaux et des matériaux et finalement l'obtention d'un comfort maximum du home pourraient rester stériles"* (De Koninck 1931: 105–6).

26. English translation of: *"Les ménagères ne sont plus des esclaves . . . Dans les locaux clairs, aux placards mécanisés, aux appareils nets et précis en connection les uns avec les autres, le travail s'est enfin synchronisé. Et l'harmonie règne! Moins lasse, plus tôt libre, mieux parée, la ménagère travaille sans rancune. Par l'organisation, par le plan, le surménage, l'irascibilité, voire la neurasthénie ont été chassés du logis"* (Gilles 1936: 563).

27. English translation of: *"Orgeuil de la bonne maîtresse de maison, autant que de la servante, la cuisine moderne, propre, élégante, est une assurance de bonne humeur et une perpétuelle source d'économie"* (X 1935b: 351–2).

28. "Pillarization" is the term used in Belgian social history to indicate the fact that social life was strictly determined by the ideological group to which one belonged: catholic, socialist or liberal. In particular, the catholic network was structured in such a way—with schools, youth movements, women's organizations, men's clubs, church activities, hospitals, unions, . . . —that a catholic person would hardly ever need to get involved with a non-catholic.

29. English translation of: *"Servis par leur naturel esprit de méthode et de leur sens d'ordre, les architectes modernes devaient fixer très vite les principes de l'organisation pratique des cuisines, qu'il s'agisse de la cuisine des pauvres ou du riche. L'une et l'autre pouvant être également économiques, hygiéniques et commodes"* (Gilles 1931: 888).

30. From the end of the nineteenth century onwards, it became more and more difficult in most European countries to find appropriate domestic servants. Due to a growing number of well-to-do people, the demand for servants continued to rise, whereas working conditions in industry and agriculture had become more attractive for younger girls. Moreover, as a result of the democratization process, the idea of "serving" and the required obedience that went with it became less self-evident (De Maeyer and Van Rompaey 1996).

31. This politically neutral grouping fought for the complete political, legal, and economic development of the woman (De Weerdt 1980: 133; Van Molle 1994: 113).

32. English translation of: *"Alles is aardig, juist iets zoals men reeds lang zocht, maar de keuken . . . daar mankeert nogal eens het een en ander aan! Niet alleen de jonge onervaren vrouwetjes letten te weinig op bouw en inrichting van de keuken, ook de meer ervaren huismoeders nemen het laatst notitie van de keuken"* (X 1935a).

33. English translation of: "... *c'est cependant autour de la cuisine que pivote toute la vie d'un ménage, et, que cette pièce soit bien ou mal agencée, qu'elle soit plaisante à occuper ou triste et sombre, c'est là que s'élaboreront les repas: et n'oubliez pas que c'est de ceux-ci que dépend une grande partie de votre bonne ou de votre mauvaise humeur*" (Guerin 1937a: 16).

34. English translation: "*Pour ma part, si les circonstances voulaient que je fusse obligée d'occuper une maison à cuisine-cave, j'aimerais mieux sacrifier un salon que accepter d'enfouir sous terre mon laboratoire culinaire*" (Guerin 1937a: 16).

35. *La femme Belge* was the organ of the Secrétariat des oeuvres Sociales Féminines Chrétiennes (Secretariat for Social Feminine Christian Works). The social Christian movement strove for better social, economic, and living conditions for the workmen's wives and their families. It promoted the ideal of "the mother at the fireside" whose ideal life consisted of the art to enjoy the triple love: love of the child, love of the husband, and devotion to the domestic hearth. They strove for the expulsion of women from the labor market, being wife and mother was considered the natural task of a woman. The exception was the unmarried woman, for whom the requirement of "equal wage for equal work" was defended (De Weerdt 1980: 105, 141, 158; Van Molle 1994: 157).

36. The Nationaal Verbond van Christelijke Vrouwengilden (National League of Christian Women's Guilds), that addressed working-class women and in which the different Catholic women's guilds were united, was established in 1920 and shared the Catholic opinion considering the woman. The natural task of the woman was being a wife and mother, so one strove for a restriction or abolition of women's labor. Vrouwenbeweging was a Flemish organ of this Union (its Walloon counterpart was La Ligue des Femmes) and had as target group the members of the K.A.V., the Katholieke Arbeidersvrouwen (Catholic Working-class Women) (De Weerdt 1980: 141, 158; Van Molle 1995: 326–30).

37. It was only at the end of the 1930s that an article about (electric or gas) cookers was published in Vrouwenbeweging, so one can assume that it didn't belong at all to the living environment of the members of the K.A.V. during the interwar period. Magazines of the early 1930s addressing women of the middle classes, on the other hand, already dealt with cookers as if they were something rather taken for granted. (V. M. 1938: 10–11).

38. English translation of: "*Niet alleen omdat alles er net en verzorgd is. Niet alleen omdat moeder er voor een goed vuurtje zorgt. Niet alleen omdat we er eten vinden. Maar ook omdat we er elkaar terugvinden ... Och, ik kan niet goed zeggen waarom: we zijn daar thuis—en dat is al!*" (X) 1939a: 16.

39. The Boerinnenbond (Women Farmers' Association) was established in 1911 as a central department of the Boerenbond (Farmers' Association), with the support of the well-off Catholic circles and the clergy. The main aim of this organization of catholic women farmers was the foundation of new women farmers' guilds and the incorporation of already existing guilds. The Boerinnenbond wanted mainly to impart expert knowledge to the women farmers. Seeing that from c. 1930 the Boerinnenbond took the whole parish, and not only the farmer's class, as its working area, frictions with the K.A.V. (Catholic Working-class Women) arose. De Boerin was the Flemish organ of the Boerinnenbond. (De Weerdt 1980: 105; Van Molle 1995: ii).

40. The consulted magazines are *Stem der Vrouw* and *La Famille Prévoyante*. *Stem der Vrouw* was the organ of the Socialistische Vrouwenbeweging (Socialistic Women's Movement) and since 1922 of the Socialistische Vooruitziende Vrouwen (Socialistic Far-sighted Women). The Socialistische Vrouwenbeweging gave women the free choice between housewife or wage laborer. A combination of marriage, motherhood, and paid work was considered as the ideal. So, here too one idealized the mother function of a woman, although not to the same extent as the catholics. In order to win more women of the working class over to socialism, in 1922 the mutuality Socialistische Vooruitziende Vrouwen was established. Joining a mutuality

meant, after all, social improvements. It tried to get through to both house-wives and working women. Since 1923, the mutuality became the most important socialist women's organization. *La Famille Prévoyante* was also a mouthpiece of the socialistic mutualities. (De Weerdt 1980: 142–7, 1997: 104; Van Molle 1994, 1995: 241–52).

41. Looking at the type-plans from several housing societies for working-class houses, one can assume that these societies can be rated among those "pragmatics:" generally only small changes in the plans were carried out during those years (Vlaamse Huisvestingsmaatschappij Brussel 1997: 356–7; Société Nationale d'Habitation et Logements à Bon Marché sd).

42. For the evolution in the type-plans for workmen's houses, constructed by the Belgian National Company for low-rent dwellings (Nationale Maatschappij voor Goedkope Woningen) established in 1919a, see Vlaamse Huisvest-ingsmaatschappij Brussel 1997: 353–8.

43. English translation of: "*La cuisine primitive de nos grand'mères a évolué au point de devenir un véritable laboratoire: placards encastrés, armoire frigorifique, évier-bassin pourvu d'eau chaude et froide, foyer au gaz ou à l'electricité, porte-savon, porte-allumettes, vide-poubelle, etc., constituent dorénavant l'ameublement typique de ce local utile*" (Collin, 1936: 503).

44. English translation of: "*. . . la cuisine doit être suffucamment grande pour contenir à l'aise tout l'équipement et permettre une circulation facile, et suffucamment petite pour interdire son utilisation comme salle à manger. L'utilisation de la cuisine pour prendre des repas est une très mauvaise habitude, qui, hélas! est profondement ancrée en Belgique*" Delhaye 1946: 113).

45. English translation of: "*Lors de l'acquisition d'un appartement, le bon père de famille veillera à ce que la cuisine soit parfaite, ou susceptible par des transformations de le devenir. Il assura ainsi à la ménagère les facilités ausquelles elle a droit, et indirectement on récoltera des multiples avantages*" Delhaye 1946: 111).

46. English translation of: "*De plus en plus, les nécessités des temps nous imposent pour l'habitation bourgeoise 'the one made's home,' où le service peut être assuré par une seule bonne, ce qui entraîne une simplification de plus en plus grande de l'habitat*" De Ridder 1925: 403).

47. Compare the comments made by the tenants of Kensal House in London, quoted by Elisabeth Darling: "Thirty-two tenants [out of 68] said they would like a larger kitchen, while 37 said they would eat in the kitchen if it were larger. The problem was that the desire of the designers to separate the activities of cooking and living was in conflict with the way the tenants wanted to live their lives. One tenant explained: 'We nearly always eat in the kitchen so as to keep the sitting room tidy.' This response was a common one. Tenants did not like the fact that they had only one living space" (Darling 2000: 172).

REFERENCES

B. J. 1933. "Het Hoekje van den Man—schab voor kastrollen." *Vrouwenbeweging* 20(15): 86.

B. J. 1937. "Keukenkastjes." *Vrouwenbeweging* no. 8 (August 1937): 16.

B. J. 1939. "Zitten." *Vrouwenbeweging* no. 1 (January 1939): 22–3.

Beer, Ingeborg. 1994. *Architektur für den Alltag—vom sozialen und frauen-orientierten Anspruch der Siedlungsarchitektur der zwanziger Jahre.* Berlin: Schelzky & Jeep.

Bervoets, Liesbeth. 1998. "Maatschappelijk transformaties in bouwen en wonen." *Tijdschrift voor genderstudies* 1(3): 23–30.

Bourgeois, Victor. 1930. "IIème Congrès International d'Architecture Moderne (Francfort–sur-Main 24–26 Octobre 1929): Le Programme de l'habitation minimum—Rapport présenté par l'Architecte Victor Bourgeois (Bruxelles)." *Tekhné* 3(8): 115–29.

Bourguet, Henriette. 1934. "A l'exposition de l'habitation: un aménagement harmonieux et pratique." *Femmes d'aujourd'hui* no. 64 (June 1934): 15.

Cieraad, Irene. 1998. "Het huishouden tussen droom en daad: over de toekomst van de keuken." Ruth Oldenziel and Carolien Bouw (eds) *Schoon genoeg—Huisvrouwen en huishoudtechnologie in Nederland 1898–1998*, pp. 31–57. Nijmegen: SUN.

Collin, Jean-F. 1936. "De l'évolution de l'habitation en fonction de la civilisation domestique." *Bâtir* 5(38): 503–5.

Darling, Elizabeth. 2000. "'What the Tenants think of Kensal House': Experts' Assumptions versus Tenants' Realities in the Modern Home." *Journal of Architectural Education* 53(2): 167–77.

De Koninck, L.-H. 1930. "Type et procédé de construction d'une habitation rationnelle—architecte: L. H. De Koninck." *La Cité* 4: 1–12.

De Koninck, L.-H. 1931. "La cuisine standard industrialisée." *La Cité* 9(9): 105–18.

De Koninck, L.-H. 1933. "La standardisation dans l'équipement de cuisines modernes en Belgique." *La Technique des Travaux* 9(12): 732–6.

De Maeyer, Jan and Lies Van Rompaey (eds). 1996. *Upstairs, Downstairs: Dienstpersoneel in Vlaanderen 1750–1995*. Gent: Provinciebestuur Oost-Vlaanderen.

De Meulder, Bruno, Pascal De Decker, Karina Van Herck, Michael Ryckewaert and Helena Vansteelant. 1999. "Over de plaats van de volkswoningbouw in de Vlaamse ruimte." In Peeters, Leo (ed.) *Huiszoeking: een kijkboek sociale woningbouw*, pp. 10–80. Brussels: Ministerie van de Vlaamse Gemeenschap (Binnenlandse aangelegenheden, stedelijk beleid & huisvesting).

De Ridder, A. 1925. "Maisons d'habitation construite: Boulevard St-Michel, 115, Bruxelles." *La Technique des Travaux* 1(11–12): 403–5.

De Weerdt, Denise. 1980. *En de vrouwen? Vrouw, vrouwenbewegingen en feminisme in België (1830–1960)*. Gent: Masereelfonds.

De Weerdt, Denise (ed.). 1997. *De Dochters van Marianne, 75 jaar SVV*. Antwerp: Uitgeverij Hadewijch.

Deletang, Maurice. 1936. "La maison de maître moderne selon l'architecte Anversois Rik Jacops." *Bâtir* 5(49): 967.

Deletang, Maurice. 1937. "Immeuble d'appartement à Anderlecht." *Bâtir* 7(61): 1503

Delevoy, R-L, M. Culot and M. Gierst (eds). 1980. *L. H. De Koninck*. Brussels: Archives d'architecture moderne.

Delhaye, Jean. 1946. *L'appartement d'aujourd'hui*. Luik: Editions Desoer.

Droesbeke Cocq, Made. 1935. "Interieur." *Egalité* 5(17): 17–18.

Duykers, Victor. 1933. "A propos de la petite habitation bourgeoise . . . l'habitation moyenne est fonctionnelle." *Bâtir* 2(11): 414–18.

Flouquet, P.-L. 1933. "L'habitation fonctionnelle, une solution de l'architecte L-H De Koninck." *Bâtir* 2(6): 220–2.

Flouquet, P.-L. 1936. "Une habitation 'solaire.'" *Bâtir* 5(46): 845–6.

Gaspard, Maurice. 1933. "Pour l'hygiène de la ménagère: la cuisine et l'office." *Bâtir* 2(4): 146–8.

Gilles, Pierre. 1932. "Le confort moderne: la cuisine electrifiée." *Bâtir* 1(23): 888–91.

Gilles, Pierre. 1936. "Le plan: maître de la cuisine." *Bâtir* 5(39): 562–3.

Guerin, Thérèse. 1937a. "Les Cuisines Modernes." *Chez Soi* no. 17 (May 1937): 16–17.

Guerin, Thérèse 1937b. "Les Cuisines Modernes: la disposition rationelle des meubles de cuisine." *Chez Soi* no. 20 (August 1937): 18–19.

Henderson, Susan R. 1996. "A Revolution in the Woman's sphere: Grethe Lihotzky and the Frankfurt Kitchen." In Debra Carol, Elizabeth Danze, and Carol Henderson (eds) *Architecture and Feminism*, pp. 221–53. New York: Princeton Architectural Press.

Helin, M.-C. and J. Hubeaux. 1936. "Petite chronique de l'organisation ménagère: Mouvements et gestes de la ménagères." *Chez Soi* no. 9 (September 1936): 31–2.

Hennaut, Eric. 1996. "De bloei van het appartementsgebouw." In Maurice Culot (ed.) *Art Deco architectuur—Brussel 1920–1930*, pp. 75–85. Brussels: AAM.

Henrotin, Claire. 1932a. "La construction rationnelle de la cuisine moderne: Définition de la cuisine et des opérations qui s'y effectuent." *Bulletin Ergologique (Annexe mensuelle au Bulletin du Comité National Belge de l'Organisation Scientifique)* 2(6): 23.

Henrotin, Claire. 1932b. "Le Mobilier rationnel de la Cuisine moderne (1er article)." *Bulletin Ergologique (Annexe mensuelle au Bulletin du Comité National Belge de l'Organisation Scientifique)*2(10): 43–4.

Henrotin, Claire. 1932c. "Le Mobilier rationnel de la Cuisine moderne (2° article)." *Bulletin Ergologique (Annexe mensuelle au Bulletin du Comité National Belge de l'Organisation Scientifique)* 2(12): 51–4.

Henrotin, Claire. 1933. "Le Mobilier rationnel de la Cuisine moderne (3° article)." *Bulletin Ergologique (Annexe mensuelle au Bulletin du Comité National Belge de l'Organisation Scientifique)* 3(3): 9–10.

Heyman, Alice. 1935. "Het electrische huishouden." *De stem der vrouw: maandblad der socialistische vooruitziende vrouwen* 25(4): 1–2.

Hoste, Huib. 1928. "Het woningvraagstuk." *Opbouwen* 1(3): 133–9.

Hoste, Huib.1937. "Iets over keukens." *Opbouwen* no. 5 (1937): 76–9.

Japsenne, Angéline. 1929. "La Maison 'minimum.'" *La femme Belge* no. 9 (November 1929): 533–7.

Japsenne, Angéline. 1930. "A propos de l'habitation minimum." *La femme Belge* no. 10 (December 1930): 580–6.

Japsenne, Angéline. 1931. "Le travail ménager de la femme." *La femme Belge* nos 4–5 (April–May 1931): 236–41.

Jasinski, Stanislas.1939. "L'Architecte en le Maître de l'ouvrage." *Clarté. art et art décoratif. achitecture* 12(8): XIII–XXXII.

J. W. 1935. "Eene plaats voor elk voorwerp en alles op zijn plaats." *De Boerin* 23(8): 239.

Martha. 1938. "In moeders keuken is het goed: De schouw onzer keuken." *Vrouwenbeweging*, no. 4 (April 1938): 17–19.

Matant. 1928. "Over keukenkasten." *De Boerin* 16(1): 7–9.

M. L. 1920. "Ons huis: Hoe maken we ons huis aangenaam?" *De Boerin* 8(5): 70–2.

Nicht Boub. 1926. "Moderne huishouding." *Het Modeblad voor het huisgezin* 2(38): 7.

Puissant, A. 1931. *L'Habitation ouvrière: La nouvelle cité-jardin de Couillet.* Brussels: Van Keerberghen.

Rogister, Victor. 1935. "L'organisation de l'appartement." *La Technique des Travaux* 11(10): 527–30.

Rombaut, Emile. 1924. "Inrichting en verzorging der woning." *Ontwikkeling en Uitspanning* 2(11): 168–9.

Ruëgg, Arthur. 1989. "La contribution de De Koninck à 'l'habitation nouvelle.'" In Caroline Mierop and Anne Van Loo (eds) *Louis Herman De Koninck: Architecte des années modernes/Architect of modern times*, pp. 187–216. Brussels: Archives d'architecture moderne.

S.S. 1934a. "Rationalisation ménagère." *Egalité* 1(21): 9–13.

S.S. 1934b. "La Rationalisation Ménagère." *Egalité* 2(22–3): 43–8.

Segalen, Martine. 1994. "The Salon des Arts Ménagers, 1923–1983: A French Effort to Instil the Virtues of Home and the Norms of Good Taste." *Journal of Design History* 7(4): 267–75.

Seroen, F. 1928. "A propos d'habitation." *L'Habitation à Bon Marché* 8(2): 21–31.

Smets, Marcel. 1977. *De ontwikkeling van de tuinwijkgedachte in België: Een overzicht van de Belgische volkswoningbouw/1830–1930.* Brussels: Pierre Mardaga.

Société Nationale d'Habitation et Logements à Bon Marché (ed.). SD. *Album de plans-types/Album van modelplannen van L'Habitation à Bon Marché*, (boek1). Brussels: Société Nationale d'Habitation et Logements à Bon Marché.

Van Der Woud, Auke. 1983. *Het nieuwe bouwen internationaal. CIAM. Volkshuisvesting. Stedenbouw.* Delft: Delft University Press.

Van Loo, Anne and Frederica Zampa. 1994. "Modern versus harmonie." In R. Gobyn and W. Spriet (eds) *De jaren '30 in België. De massa in verleiding*, pp. 197–217. Brussels: ASLK.

Van Molle, Leen. 1994. *Répertoire des sources pour l'histoire des femmes en Belgique: Tome I: Répertoire de la presse féminine et féministe en Belgique 1830–1994*. Brussels: Ministerie van Arbeid en Tewerkstelling.

Van Molle, Leen. 1995. *Bronnen voor de vrouwengeschiedenis in België: deel II: Repertorium van de feministische en de vrouwenpers 1830–1994*. Brussels: Ministerie van Arbeid en Tewerkstelling.

Vandenbreeden, Jos and France Vanlaethem. 1996. *Art Deco en Modernisme in België: Architectuur in het Interbellum*. Tielt: Lannoo.

Vlaamse Huisvestingsmaatschappij Brussel (ed.). 1997. *Bouwstenen van sociaal woningbeleid '45–'95: De VHM bekijkt 50 jaar volkshuisvesting in Vlaanderen*, 2 vols. Brussels: VHM.

V. M. 1938. Koken we 's zomens . . . zonder gebruik te moeten maken van ons keukenfornuis?" *Vrouwenbeweging* no. 6 (June 1938): 10–11.

Wilke, Margrith. 1998. "Kennis en kunde: Handboeken voor huisvrouwen." In Ruth Oldenziel and Carolien Bouw (eds) *Schoon Genoeg: Huisvrouwen en huishoudtechnologie in Nederland 1898–1998*, pp. 59–90. Nijmegen: SUN.

X. 1927. "Zelfverwarmer." *De stem der vrouw: maandblad der socialistische vooruitziende vrouwen* 17(12).

X. 1929a. "Oost West Thuis Best." *Vrouwenbeweging* 16(6): 88–9.

X. 1929. "Iets over verlichting." *Vrouwenbeweging* 16(12): 182.

X. 1932a. "Huishoudelijke opvoeding." *De stem der vrouw: maandblad der socialistische vooruitziende vrouwen* 22(4).

X. 1932b. "Groote Tentoonstelling te Boschvoorde." *Vrouwenbeweging* 19(5): 67.

X. 1932c. "Le froid ménager." *Bâtir* 1(1): 32–3.

X. 1932d. "Oost West Thuis Best—De kunst om te werken zonder u te vermoeien." *Vrouwenbeweging* 19(6): 86.

X. 1933. "Naar meer familieleven." *Vrouwenbeweging* 20(2): 26–7.

X. 1934a. "Des idées pratiques pour la cuisine." *Femmes d'aujourd'hui* no. 49 (March 1934): 14.

X. 1934b. "Rationaliseering van de huishouding." *De Boerin* 22(5): 141–2.

X. 1935a. "Een praktische keukeninrichting." *Het Rijk der Vrouw* no. 13 (30 March 1935).

X. 1935b. "Le laboratoire des délices: la cuisine." *Bâtir* 4(34): 351–2.

X. 1936. "L'habitation: la décoration du foyer." *La Famille Prévoyante* January 1936

X. 1937a. "Onze praktische keuken." *Het Rijk der Vrouw* no. 10 (6 March 1937).

X. 1937b. "La ménagère de l'avenir." *La Famille Prévoyante*, November 1937.

X. 1938a. "Ik zie niet goed . . ." *Vrouwenbeweging* no. 10 (October 1938): 16–17.

X. 1938b. "Niet vermenigvuldigen, maar vereenvoudigen." *Vrouwenbeweging* no. 11 (November 1938) 6–7.

X. 1938c. "Wij willen een familietafel." *Vrouwenbeweging* no. 12 (December 1938): 4–5.

X. 1938d. "Considération: économiques et urbanistiques concernant la 'Résidence Leopold.'" *Bâtir* no. 66 (May 1938): 158–67.

X. 1939a. "In moeders' keuken." *Vrouwenbeweging* 8(2): 16–17.

X. 1939b. "Die geen hoofd heeft moet beenen hebben." *Vrouwenbeweging* no. 3 (March 1939): 8.

X. 1939c. "Een bittere aanklacht." *Vrouwenbeweging* no. 4 (April 1939): 15.

X. 1939d. "Onze prijskampen." *Vrouwenbeweging* no. 5 (May 1939): 16.

X. 1939e. "Wij willen een familiehuis." *Vrouwenbeweging* no. 6 (June 1939): 4–5.

X. 1939f. "Wij bouwen een nieuwen thuis." *Vrouwenbeweging* no. 8 (August 1939): 4–5.

X. 1939g. "Perfection de la cuisine éléctrique." *Bâtir* 8(6): 324–5.

HOME CULTURES   VOLUME 1, ISSUE 1.
PP 51–60

REPRINTS AVAILABLE
DIRECTLY FROM THE
PUBLISHERS.

PHOTOCOPYING
PERMITTED BY LICENSE
ONLY

© BERG 2004
PRINTED IN THE UK

JEAN-SÉBASTIEN MARCOUX

BODY EXCHANGES: MATERIAL CULTURE, GENDER AND STEREOTYPES IN THE MAKING

JEAN-SÉBASTIEN MARCOUX IS
ASSISTANT PROFESSOR OF
ANTHROPOLOGY OF
CONSUMPTION, MATERIAL
CULTURE, AND CONSUMER
RESEARCH AT
HEC MONTRÉAL. HIS
CURRENT RESEARCH
INTERESTS ARE CONSUMER
SUPPORT NETWORKS, THE
PRODUCTION OF VALUE IN
THE INFORMAL SECTORS OF
MARKETING AND THE
BROADER ISSUE OF THE
"SECOND LIFE" OF THINGS.

In the line of recent works on the relationship between body and gender, this article examines the bodily investment of gender construction. Grounded in an ethnographic fieldwork, it focuses on the ways in which gender relations in North America are constructed through the manipulation of objects, via body exchanges. It shows that physicality cannot simply be taken as a given on which genders are imposed. It is used to maintain sexual differences in a normative fashion. In attempting to understand this economy of body exchanges, this article calls for a broadening of our understanding of gender stereotypes. In doing this, it challenges the idea that changes of consciousness may not have reached the level of practices. It reveals instead that people are not fooled. They may even engage into these relations with a certain degree of irony.

"A WOMAN NEEDS A MAN TO MOVE"

I became interested in the issue of gender after coming back from fieldwork in North America during which I worked on the experience of mobility. I really started to consider the issue after hearing a colleague of mine, a woman in her thirties, declare that "a woman needs a man to move." A move is such a chore, as she went on to explain, that the physical strength of a man is at the least welcomed, if not necessary. Saying that moving is a physical task giving way to a gendered division of labor does not come as a big surprise. What intrigued me in this spontaneous declaration was the implied image of gender complementarity emanating from it; something Judith Butler (1999) would certainly characterize as a "fictional" complementarity.

This article focuses on the ways in which gender roles, behaviors, and stereotypes are constructed through the manipulation of objects, especially "heavy" objects. It examines how gender roles are created and enacted in the course of physical tasks, contending that physicality acts as both the determinant and the determination of these roles. It is inspired by the recent works in consumer research on gender (Bristor and Fischer 1993; Schroeder 2003). More importantly, it can be situated in the line of contemporary material culture studies that emphasize the importance of routines, non-discursive forms of knowledge and practices embodied in objects (Kaufmann 1992; Miller 1987, 1988, 1998). These works aim to leap beyond the level of discourse and access people's practices. They show what can be gained by unveiling the principles of organization prevailing in the material world as well as what needs to be understood from the study of the manipulation of more mundane artifacts. Those knowledge and practices are difficult to grasp, however. They are difficult to accede to. Not so much because people are reluctant to face them, but because they are taken for granted or unnoticed by those using them. For Kaufmann (1992), people often have little to say about these practices. They do not talk about those gestures that apparently speak by themselves.

Starting from an ethnographic experience this article explores the economy of body exchanges taking shape through the manipulation of objects. This reflection voluntarily leaves aside the issue of class, although gender and class may be difficult to distinguish in some instances. Rather, it focuses on the phenomenological dimension of gender construction. As such, it draws upon the works of phenomenologists like Marion Young who analyzes the situatedness of the feminine body in contemporary societies, and problematizes the use of physicality. My thoughts also draw on the works of Judith Butler (1993, 1999) who emphasizes the performance of gender. I also take from the work of Pierre Bourdieu, of which *The Masculine Domination* (Bourdieu 1998) is particularly relevant to this study as it brings the issue of changes in consciousness in regards to gender relations at the level of practices; that is, the non-discursive level of knowledge: knowledge that is embodied. This study is founded on fieldwork conducted in Montreal among some twenty-three households, most of which were composed of women. They evolve in a society where feminism has helped achieve significant advances in the past decades. Data were collected between September 1997 and July 1999 through participant observation in which these households were accompanied throughout their move as well as assisted on the actual day. It is important to emphasize that moving is used here as a methodology (Marcoux 2002). Helping someone to move gives access to the lived experience of gender relations, and to the stereotypes in the making. It provides an access to deep social processes. Here I present how the fieldwork was conducted, and how, as a researcher, I immersed myself in people's material world by accompanying them in the physical and metaphorical journey of the move: from the moment they decided to move, to the settlement, through the move *per se*. In many instances, I was involved in the "excavation" of cluttered cupboards, basement, and chests of drawers; I sorted things with people, watched them do it as I listened to them. Moreover, I helped them move their possessions. As such, I wanted to get access to the important decisions like the choice of a location. I also wanted to accede to the small gestures that have major implications as well as those things that are hardly verbalized such as the gendered behaviors. In the text that follows, I am interested in finding out how people move rather than why they move. I analyze the actual move: Who takes part in it? What are the human and material resources mobilized? Who does what? Also, always while taking care not to introduce too many biases into my study, for the sake of clarity I devote more attention to certain more representative informants.

DEMONSTRATIONS OF STRENGTH

When Gérard Lambert[1]—a working-class man in his forties, moved with his family into a bungalow they acquired, he insisted on doing it with the help of colleagues and acquaintances instead of hiring professional movers. Mr Lambert was worried about financial issues, mortgage payments, installation work, renovation, etc. As such, he wished to save on the moving costs when he and his family acceded to ownership. The Lamberts are not alone. In a North American city like Montreal, numerous people move themselves, which lets them do it at low cost as many examples drawn from the field can testify. It may cost as few as $80, even $50, in comparison to $300, $635 and $645 when using a moving company. The local press calls these people "do-it-yourselfers" (L.J.B. 1986), "house-made movers" (Côté 1998) or "autonomous movers" (Bernard 1991). They draw on friends, relatives and colleagues as "labor." This is what is translated by expressions like "*Donner un coup d'main*" (giving a helping hand). There are few data on the number of people moving on their own due to the informal character of the activity.[2] Yet, moving has inspired popular composers like Réjean Ducharme, Robert Charlebois, Thibaud deCorta, and Polo, poets, as well as writers such as Gabrielle Roy (1945). Moving is still characterized—sometimes sarcastically, other times humorously—as the Montrealers' "national sport" (Alarie 1997; Nadeau 1994). It is perceived as a "hobby" (Neko 1999) or as a part of the "usual razzmatazz" (Dion 1993). Some even describe it as a "local ritual," "an event that, like sex, snow and smoked meat, transcends the barriers of language" (Abley 1996: 52).

I should say that in a city like Montreal moving around is institutionalized. Most of the people move at about the same time. The leases are often fixed term leases of a twelve-month period beginning on the 1st of July so that most people move on that day (Figure 1). This even pinched the curiosity of the BBC in London which produced a documentary on the event in 1998.[3] What makes moving interesting, however, is how it occurs. On moving day, Mr Lambert took care of moving the furniture, the appliances, and the family's possessions with the help of Patrick, his sixteen-year-old son and two friends of Patrick of about the same age. Mr Lambert also got some help from one of his work colleagues (a man in his forties) who brought his pick-up truck and his son, a boy aged fourteen or fifteen. The moving of possessions lasted the whole day. During most of that time, Mme Lambert (forty-two years old) disappeared. She who had patiently been preparing her family's move for three months, she who packed everything, sorted things out, and cleaned them literally shied away on moving day only to reappear at lunch. She confined herself to preparing the meal for the people who came to give a hand and let her husband, along with the other men, move their possessions. As far as I could observe, men often take care of heavy things on the moving day. Some like Gérard Lambert do so in a protective, paternalistic fashion, claiming that things like the refrigerator are too heavy for women, that they could hurt themselves. "Move on, let me handle it . . ." we might hear. In certain instances, women also voluntarily leave the place to men because of age, back problems, or because they believe it is not appropriate for them, as is the case of Mme Lambert. Others are also simply excluded. Mr Lambert insisted on Florence, his eighteen-year-old daughter, leaving the stage like her mother had when came the time to handle the refrigerator. Florence was pushed aside. Her father preferred to see the men handling it even though they were aged sixteen, fifteen, even fourteen!

Florence was pushed aside though she felt fully capable of handling the refrigerator and other appliances and claimed the right to do so; and I use the word "right" on purpose because handling the refrigerator appears to be more

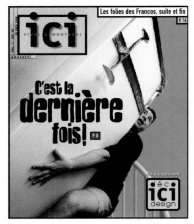

Figure 1
Cover page of *Ici Montreal*, a free cultural magazine distributed every week. The issue published on June 25, 1998 is devoted to moving day. It can be translated as "Never Again." Reproduced with the permission of the editor.

like a privilege than a task to fulfill in these cases. Florence reacted with anger after being excluded. She simply refused the physical role to which her father and her brother wanted to confine her: the handling of the "light" things, the cleaning of the kitchen, the fixing of the meal for the movers; a role her mother accepted without demur. In doing this, she incurred her father's wrath, the sarcastic remarks of her brother, and came against her mother's incomprehension.

GENDER PERFORMANCES AND THE EFFECT OF NATURALNESS
The women that I observed and followed in the course of my fieldwork commonly take care of the areas of the move that remain hidden: the cleaning of the kitchen, of the refrigerator, of the cupboards, and of the bathroom. More often, they also care for the children. Maria and her friends, for instance, four middle-class women in their forties who work in education and in the cultural industry helped a girlfriend to move after a separation. Maria and her friends who could be described as non-radical feminists insisted on being present on moving day, claiming that their friend would be crazy to try to handle the move alone. They contended that a way of relieving her would be to help her settle in as quickly as possible. They wished to be there and accompany their friend, which could be read as a willingness to support her morally in a difficult moment. They took care of cleaning the new apartment from the top to the bottom while the "guys"—among whom I was, moved the things. They divided the tasks between themselves. Maria washed up the walls and ceilings of the whole apartment, Mercedes cleaned up the washroom, Constance took care of cleaning the kitchen cupboards, Clara dealt with the bedrooms, etc. Maria and her friends accepted to handle the cleaning as long they felt they were helping their friend. Afterwards, they reflected ironically on this division of tasks however, declaring that for them, women, it is "so natural" to clean up. Still, they accepted to do the cleaning as long as they were not reduced to it. Not only that they did not seek any valorization from it, they wished it to remain unnoticed.

People like Maria and her friends want to pass unnoticed. Others like Mme Lambert who played a central role in the preparation of the move remained unappreciated. As a matter of fact, as one could read in a popular American magazine: "As any woman who's ever moved can tell you, moving is women's work—that category of invisible labor, such as doing laundry, that no one notices unless it doesn't get done . . ." (Langford Carter 1982: 22). In the heat of the moment, no grand discourse presides over the sexual division of tasks. On the contrary, aside from a few cases, the attribution of responsibilities often goes without saying, as if it were taken for granted. If the division of roles is ever verbalized, it takes the form of gendered jokes. A certain dose of derision may even prevail here, as in the case of Maria and her friends who reflect ironically on the naturalness of the division of labor. People are not fooled, since the use of irony tends to undermine the belief in natural differences. Beyond discourse, however, the division of tasks which goes without saying becomes a means for maintaining sexual differences in a normative fashion, for keeping each sex in its place, within a fictional opposition of genders. Such an opposition asserts itself all the more strongly that it is still borrowing on the effect of naturalness, on biological evidence and a certain idea of science. As Laqueur (1990) points out, science does not simply investigate. It also constitutes. As such, it rationalizes and legitimizes distinctions of sex just as much as those of race and class to the disadvantage of the powerless. In his history of the making of sex, Laqueur recalls that since the end of the eighteenth century the dominant view was that of two incommensurable and opposing sexes acting as the basis for different views of gender roles. Biology became the epistemic foundation for prescriptive claims about social order, not to say "gender order." Though gender is never fully undetermined (Butler 1993), we can hardly assume that a gendered set of behaviors may flow from biological or sexual differences (Broch-Due 1993; Miller 1988). If there are differences between men and women, these difference are not due *so much*, and I quote Marion Young: "to brute muscular strength, but to the way each sex *uses* the body in approaching tasks" (Young 1989: 56; italics in the original text).

Young's work is relevant inasmuch as it focuses on physical acts like throwing and "those sorts of bodily activities which relate to the comportment or orientation of the body as a whole, which entail gross movement, or which require the enlistment of strength and the confrontation of the body's capacities and possibilities with the resistance and malleability of things" (Young 1989: 53). She focuses on knowledge, habits, and orientations that are literally speaking "embodied." In doing this, she is able to move beyond anatomical and physiological considerations. As such, she meets Grosz (1994) for whom it is important to contest not only the domination of the body by biological terms but also the terms of biology itself. Young argues that a feminine body typically underuses its real capacities. She contends that women often tend to approach a physical engagement with things with timidity, uncertainty and hesitancy. They often lack confidence that they have the capacity to do what must be done. They are often unconfident towards physical tasks, which could explain their reluctance to handle heavy objects like the refrigerator. More than men, women would tend to underestimate their physical capacities. Young's argument is far from being simply psychological or essentialist. She rather identifies an "inhibited intentionality" as one of the modalities of feminine motility in contemporary societies. In a *Beauvoirienne* (deBeauvoir 1949) tradition, she insists on the fact that women learn to under-use their body; the biological discourse becoming a self-fulfilling prophecy. They learn a particular style of body behavior from an early age, as they acquire walking habits, as they learn how to sit, how to stand, etc. Young girls actively learn to hamper their movements. They develop a bodily timidity that increases with age and which varies according to social classes (I would add). Her argument takes on its full strength when insisting on "the way each sex uses the body" (Young 1989: 56). As such, it seems to echo Butler's work (1993) on the performativity of the body and the physicality operating as a norm. Yet, as one woman informant put it, "One does not need to be strong, but intelligent to lift a refrigerator."

As much as women may be uncertain about their possibilities as Young would argue, men, for their part, show little uncertainty when comes the time to handle the refrigerator. When their reputation is in peril, more often they display bravado. Above all, they never emphasize the importance of intelligence for handling a refrigerator. The issue behind the manipulation of objects and the demonstration of strength is that this represents a way of defining what is appropriate or not for each sex. For handling heavy objects (or not), displaying assurance (or not) is also part of what is considered appropriate for a woman or a man. Similarly, the rejection of a particular form of engagement with objects may become a type of contestation, not to say "subversion" of a sexual order. Interestingly, when discussing this article publicly, a woman declared to me that moving refrigerators without the help of men was often for lesbian people of her community tinted with the color of pride and victory. I do not possess enough data to push this line of argument further. Using this anecdote, however, I wish to stress that Florence's determination to help with the handling of heavy items such as the refrigerator may be perceived as a refusal to perform according to a given norm; the refrigerator becoming the bone of contention of that norm.

THE RELATIONAL CHARACTER OF GENDER RELATIONS

Perhaps, one shortcoming of Young's argument is that it fails to recognize the relational character of the gendered use of physicality. It tends to consider the feminine body in isolation. A move may become a locus of power struggle and domination: women may be invited not to transfer heavy things, they may be encouraged not to do so, pushed aside or excluded as we have seen earlier. Power relations take shape in spaces around objects. Men may block entries, take possession of the staircase, behave in intimidating ways, and push women in the backdrop as a result. As a matter of fact, a move is never de-spatialized. The anthropological literature is useful here. Miller (1998), for instance, examines how gender identity is developed relationally, in the course of shopping activities around the notions of love and sacrifice. Miller's (1988) analysis of the relational dimension of gender is even more pervasive in his discussion of the appropriation of kitchens in a North London Council through exchanges of work and advice regarding decoration and refurbishment. In examining how gender relations come into existence via a logic of exchange that is documented in Melanesian anthropology (Strathern 1988), Miller challenges the essentialist view of genders as separate entities. In a similar vein, Broch-Due (1993) emphasizes how Turkana people constitute themselves through one, two, or even three genders. As such, we can suggest that genders are not *a priori* given. They are rather constructed through the cultural development of relational forms.

Just as much as Miller finds that women do not hesitate to undertake physical work when no men are available, the young women that I followed could more easily undertake physical tasks in the absence of men. These women who are unable or unwilling to engage in exchange relationships are not so much worried about their own lack of physical capacities as one could expect when reading Young. They are rather concerned not to impose the moving of heavy things like the kitchen appliances, the washing and drying machines onto the people they care for. They are concerned about these heavy items in terms of social implications and responsibilities, requiring efforts, and entailing risks. In fact, women's concern for physical capacities particularly tends to emerge in the presence of men. Behind the illusion of gender complementarity (Butler 1999) which sends us back to a fictional heterosexist regime, physical performances on the occasions of a move, exchanges of physical help, not to say body exchanges help produce and reproduce gender stereotypes which in turn provide a meaningful structure for gender relations. Miller's work is useful as much as it emphasizes how genders are constructed through exchange of work. The limit of the comparison is that here, what is at issue, is a form of exchange marked by power relations and intimidation. If we followed Bourdieu (1998) instead, we could argue that women apparently accept these relations of domination, by adopting what he calls the categories of the dominator, and by making these categories appear as if they were natural. An example is the discourse on physical strength in which there is the idea that men may be naturally stronger, and should therefore take care of the refrigerator. Bourdieu's analysis is interesting inasmuch as it allows us to understand how cultural dispositions may be naturalized, and incorporated; sometimes deeply in the body. It shows that such dispositions do not need to be conscious to be efficient. This is illustrated well by Kaufmann's (1992) observations on the construction of the couple through domestic work, on how small intimate gestures set themselves up as obstacles in achieving equality. It tends to show that it would be facile to believe that these dispositions may be overcome simply via changes of consciousness. Bourdieu, however, fails to capture fully the logic of complicity I have often noticed operating here.

The women encountered in the course of this ethnography often accepted to ensure the cleaning of the kitchen, the cupboards, the toilet, and other hidden tasks, without necessarily feeling dominated, as long as it remained unnoticed. In some cases, such a gendered division of roles is constrained, not to say imposed upon women. Men often feel invested with the duty to care for the heavy objects, and, we can suppose, for their women counterparts. This supports Young's argument about the immanence of women's existence: women becoming mere objects. Nonetheless, the fact remains that this division of tasks is also often accepted with a certain complicity, as the feminist geographer Nancy Duncan (1996) would say. As if women voluntarily shied away from the heaviest items in order to leave the front stage to the men, to let them feel that they are still important, that they still mattered. As if they wanted to let men think that handling the heavy things makes them essential in a sense. If taking care of the heavy things like the refrigerator provides men with a sense of being necessary, it secures them in a nostalgic fashion because relying on physical strength is securing and does not require them to reconsider gender roles. As a matter of fact, it is worth asking who is really alienated.

THE POWER OF IRONY

The philosopher Judith Butler (1993, 1999) demonstrates the fictional character of discrete and polar gender categories. Butler criticizes the binary frames through which gender is conceptualized and the illusion of stability of those frames, not to speak of the illusion of complementarity. For her, gender is an act that requires a performance which is repeated over time on mundane and public occasions; a stylized repetition of bodily gestures. Moving is an event during which gender relations and the fiction of complementarity are performed as such. It entails a strong normalization of the use of physical strength, and it reproduces it. Moving pertains to the domain of practices, acts and bodily comportments enlisting physical strength during which gender relations are created and enacted. It reminds us how physicality cannot simply be taken as a given on which genders are imposed. It is used, as in this case, to maintain sexual differences in a normative fashion; to challenge them on occasion, even transform them. Indeed, a move does not only reinforce gender relations, it may also become the opportunity to contest them. It is worth mentioning that at the end of the day Florence finally earned the right to handle heavy possessions along with her brother. She also gained a new status on that occasion. Her relationship with her father was never the same again.

In attempting however, to understand how the economy of body exchanges may pervade, we could consider whether changes in consciousness have reached the level of practices. In Bourdieu's line of thought (Bourdieu 1979; Bourdieu and Wacquant 1992; Wacquant 2000), gendered relations that are embodied into practices would resurface at the time of the move, in a crisis context, despite a feminist ideology and a belief in gender equality shared by many middle-class informants. In other words, changes of consciousness would only acquire their efficacy once they have reached the level of practices; once they moved beyond the discursive level and reached Merleau-Ponty's (1945) locus of subjectivity: the body. This line of reasoning is limitative however, for it assumes the inevitability of men's prominence; an assumption challenged by Strathern (1988). For Strathern, we must stop thinking that an opposition between male and female must be about the control of men and women over each other. She calls for a greater recognition of the importance of non-hierarchical relations such as, I would say, relations of complicity. Strathern's reflection is based upon the study of Melanesian gender relations. Still, it is relevant for the purpose of our discussion because it breaks with the enduring Western assumption that femaleness is to be understood as a by-product of, or produced by, what is established as the socially dominant form, that is: maleness.

The situation described here contrasts with the feminist claim of the 1960–1970s, the idea that women are basically no different from men, and have the ambition to perform the same roles. As Catterall et al. (2000: 4) report, "differences between males and females were often played down for fear that these would be used as arguments to stifle women's progress." This is captured well by the slogan: "Anything you can do, I can do better, or at least as well." A paradigm shift colloquially referred to "Third wave feminism" which sees no necessary contradiction between romanticism and empowerment, could then explain the division of roles commonly observed here. It is an orientation characterized by self-reflexivity and irony. As a matter of fact, against Bourdieu's claim, we must acknowledge that people are not always fooled. In contrast to Kaufmann's observations, they do not necessarily delude themselves. They are often aware of the stereotypical character in the division of tasks as well as of the roles in which they operate. Many of them are even ironic. Although irony is hard to interpret since it is never clear whether it is serious or not (Brooks 2003), it provides a means in a sense to defuse a controversial situation, not to say a source of contradictions. When coupled with irony, performed humorously, these gender relations appear to remain unimportant. In other words, it is misleading to search the rationale for the resurgence of stereotypical gender relations in a gap between consciousness and practices. Instead we need to account for how people produce and reproduce stereotypes, and how those stereotypes may provide interstices between consciousness and practices in which gender relations are negotiated.

A philosophical question arises here as to the capacity to extract the social phenomenon from the material context of their occurrence. This article reveals the need to interact with people while they, themselves, interact with objects. It shows how gender roles and stereotypes take shape through the manipulation of objects as well as how objects are used in the shaping of the world. Objects do not only provide a window onto gender relations. They also help mediate those relations. The low recognition of refrigerators, the mundane aspect of the appliances and of the cleaning practices involved here is important. The futile character of these items and of the practices involving them probably gives way to a downgrading of the social patterns and gender relations emerging. As a matter of fact, these gender relations do not endure because of a lack of bodily practice since the people encountered during this fieldwork master the practices of moving. They probably persist because of a lack of recognition of the importance of the objects involved.

In any case, we need to improve our understanding of how people invest themselves into stereotypical relationships; how they "make" stereotypes, as well as how they are "made by" those stereotypes. We need to better understand how gender roles and stereotypes are permanently reproduced through the transient manipulations of material objects.

ACKNOWLEDGMENTS

The research presented here has benefited from the financial support of the Social Sciences and Human Research Council of Canada (SSHRC) as well the Royal Anthropological Institute (UK). I wish to thank Daniel Miller for his critical comments and suggestions, and Hélène Buzelin, Mélissa Gauthier, Isabelle Hanifi, and Lucy Norris for their insightful reading. Preliminary versions of this article were presented at the 6th ACR Conference on Gender, Marketing and Consumer Behavior in Dublin in June 2002 and at the 101st Annual Meeting of the American Anthropological Association in New Orleans in November 2002 in a panel organized by Haidy Geismar and Heather Horst. I would like to thank the participants of these conferences for their valuable insights and the anonymous reviewers of this article. Most of all, I wish to thank my informants for sharing their experiences with me.

NOTES

1. In order to protect the anonymity of the respondents, the names have been changed.
2. A survey conducted in June 2000 by Impact Recherche for a major telephone provider revealed that 70% of the people who moved in the Province of Quebec moved themselves (Bell Canada 2000). Survey conducted among 301 adults. The error margin is 5.6%, 19/20.
3. *Under the Sun* (BBC, 1998).

REFERENCES

Abley, Mark. 1996. "Montreal on the Move." *Canadian Geographic* 116 (July/August): 48–53.

Alarie, Marie-Hélène. 1997. "Âmes Marchandes. Rien N'arrête les Vrais Pros de la Vente de Garage." *Le Devoir* May 23.

Bell Canada. 2002. *Habitudes des Québécois à l'Occasion de leur Déménagement.* dossier 20-2034.

Bernard, Florian. 1991. "*Vade Mecum* du Parfait Déménageur." *La Presse* June 22, J2.

Bourdieu, Pierre. 1979. *La Distinction*. Paris: Éditions de Minuit.

Bourdieu, Pierre. 1998. *La Domination Masculine*. Paris: Éditions du Seuil.

Bourdieu, Pierre and Loic Wacquant. 1992. *Réponse: Pour une Anthropologie Réflexive*. Paris: Éditions du Seuil.

Broch-Due, Vigdis. 1993. "Making Meaning out of Matter: Perceptions of Sex, Gender and Bodies among the Turkana." In Vigdis Broch-Due, Ingrid Rudie and Tone Bleie (eds) *Carved Flesh/Cast Selves: Gendered Symbols and Social Practices.* pp. 53–82. Oxford: Berg.

Butler, Judith. 1993. *Bodies that Matter*. London: Routledge.

Butler, Judith. 1999. *Gender Trouble*. New York: Routledge.

Bristor, Julia M. and Eileen Fischer. 1993. "Feminist Thought: Implications for Consumer Research." *Journal of Consumer Research* 19 (March): 518–36.

Brooks, David. 2003. "The Return of the Pig: The Revival of Blatant Sexism in American Culture Has Many Progressive Thinkers Flummoxed." *The Atlantic Monthly* 291(3): 22–4.

Catterall, Myriam, Pauline Maclaran and Lorna Stevens (eds). 2000. *Marketing and Feminism. Current Issues and Research*. London: Routledge.

Côté, Hélène. 1998. "Déménagement: Pour Éviter les Mauvaises Surprises." *Consommation, le Magazine d'Information et d'Action d'Option Consommateurs.* Spring, 5–8.

deBeauvoir, Simone. 1949. *Le Deuxième Sexe*. Paris: Gallimard.

Dion, Jean. 1993. "La Fête du Canapé." *Le Devoir* June 30.

Duncan, Nancy. 1996. "Renegotiating Gender and Sexuality in Public and Private Spaces." In Nancy Duncan (ed.) *Body Space: Destabilizing Geographies of Gender and Sexuality*, pp. 127–56. London: Routledge.

Grosz, Elizabeth. 1994. *Volatile Bodies: Toward a Corporeal Feminism*. Bloomington, IN: Indiana University Press.

Kaufmann, Jean-Claude. 1992. *La Trame Conjuguale. Analyse du Couple par son Linge*. Paris: Éditions Nathan.

Langford Carter, Judy. 1982. "We've Moved." *Redbook* 159, May 22: 22–6.

Laqueur, Thomas. 1990. *Making Sex: Body and Gender from the Greeks to Freud*. London: Harvard University Press.

L.J.B. 1986. "Moving? This can Make it Easier." *Good Housekeeping* 103 (August): 188.

Marcoux, Jean-Sébastien. 2002. "Helping People to Move." Paper presented at the *Annual conference of the American Anthropological Association (AAA)*, New Orleans, LA, November.

Merleau-Ponty, Maurice. 1945. *La Phénoménologie de la Perception*. Paris: Gallimard.

Miller, Daniel. 1987. *Material Culture and Mass Consumption*. Oxford: Blackwell.

Miller, Daniel. 1988. "Appropriating the State on the Council Estate." *Man* 23: 353–72.

Miller, Daniel. 1998. *A Theory of Shopping*. Cambridge: Polity Press, Cornell University Press.

Nadeau, Jacques. 1994. "La Fête du Déménagement." *Le Devoir* July 2.

Neeko, Likongo. 1999. "Le Déménagement, un Sport Populaire." *La Presse* July 2.

Roy, Gabrielle. 1945. *Bonheur d'Occasion*, Montreal: Éditions Boréal.

Schroeder, Jonathan (ed.) 2003. "Gender and Identity, Special Issue." *Consumption, Markets and Culture* 6(1).

Strathern, Marilyn. 1988. *The Gender of the Gift*. London: University of California Press.

Young, Iris Marion. 1989. "Throwing Like a Girl: A Phenomenology of Feminine Body Comportment, Motility, and Spatiality." In Jeffner Allen and Iris Marion Young (eds) *The Thinking Muse: Feminism and Modern French Philosophers*, pp. 51–70. Bloomington, IN: Indiana University Press.

Wacquant, Loic. 2000. *Corps et Âme: Carnets Ethnographiques d'un Apprenti Boxeur*. Marseilles: Agone.

HOME CULTURES   VOLUME 1, ISSUE 1.   REPRINTS AVAILABLE   PHOTOCOPYING   © BERG 2004
                 PP 61–82   DIRECTLY FROM THE   PERMITTED BY LICENSE   PRINTED IN THE UK
                                      PUBLISHERS.   ONLY

WILLIAM J. GLOVER

"A FEELING OF ABSENCE FROM OLD ENGLAND:" THE COLONIAL BUNGALOW

WILL GLOVER IS AN ASSISTANT PROFESSOR OF ARCHITECTURAL HISTORY AT THE UNIVERSITY OF MICHIGAN.

This article explores how the colonial bungalow provided a setting for attempting to bridge perceived distances between English home life and its corollary in colonial India. At the same time, the article suggests that the bungalow gave presence to a kind of "Indian-ness," a social and material presence that produced anxiety in its European occupants. On the one hand, as the primary realm of English domesticity in India the bungalow provided a setting for the cultivation of habits of self-control thought necessary for comporting the self with authority. On the other hand, the material qualities of the bungalow's construction, along with the social practices it had to accommodate, continually worked against these goals, something discussed in British memoirs, travel accounts, and guides to household management written through-out the latter half of the nineteenth century. What tied these two disparate discourses together was the bungalow itself, as a material artifact with distinctive qualities.

> I am very much amused to witness English home life. There is no such word as "home" in our language; [in England] it is a word employed chiefly in the elevated style. And every heart is stirred by it. I had heard the word so often that I was anxious to see an English home and real home life. This is a small cozy house, tastefully furnished . . . Through-out the central parts of London there are large buildings of five or six stories, rented either by flats or rooms. In many cases these buildings are separated from the street in front by railings, with a small gate in front leading up a short flight of steps to a door which is numbered. Inside, generally, the dining room is on the ground floor, the drawing room on the first, and the bedrooms above. Beneath the ground floor are the rooms for servants and the kitchen. This is the kind of abode in which our retired Lieutenant Governors live.

> Excerpt from the London travel diary of
> Nawab Mehdi Hasan Khan, 1890.[1]

The Indian travel account quoted above highlights the "elevated" status of the English home in the minds of that island's inhabitants, just as it alludes to differences between English homes in England and English homes in colonial India. If the typical retired Lieutenant Governor's London row-house (as described by Khan) was notable for being "small" and "cozy," then the active Lieutenant Governor's residence in India at the time was certain to be a much grander affair. Not simply the residence of a loyal and well-placed government servant, such a house in India was, according to one prominent historian of British India, "a representation of the authority of an imperial power and the residence of that power's representative in the colony" (Metcalf 1989: 9).

While this may have been true for the largest official residences, it would not be true of the far humbler structures that were home to the vast majority of Europeans in colonial India. As a visible feature of the landscape, these simpler homes shared some of the symbolic rhetoric of exclusion and superiority that characterized the empire's largest residences. Most European houses were isolated from the street by walls and gates; they were set in relatively large lots; and they were often raised honorifically above their surroundings on a stepped plinth. Even simple houses were sometimes adorned with neoclassical or gothic revival ornament, features that alluded both to extra-local sources of cultural authority and to contemporary fashions in the distant metropole. But the ordinary colonial bungalow was much more than a symbolic visual form. It was also a complicated social and material milieu, the setting for a type of domesticity that was meant to help reflect and instill the values and dispositions that separated rulers from their subjects.

Many scholars have underlined the importance of a discourse on "domesticity" in the constitution of colonial power (Chatterjee 1993; Comaroff and Comaroff 1992; Hall 2002; McClintock 1995; Sinha 1995; Stoler 1995; White 1990). The Anglo-European ideal of middle-class domesticity described the home as a refuge from the competitive outside world, an incubator for the moral development of children, and a temple to conjugal sexuality. In colonial settings, the Anglo-European home was seen as both a refuge from the strange and unfamiliar world outside, and a potential catalyst for the social improvement of "Native" society. Maintaining proper domestic arrangements in the colony was seen as a bulwark against the feared dissolution of character that might come about through prolonged exposure to the tropics (Metcalf 1994: 160–185; Stoler 1995). The properly ordered home was also thought to be a powerful device for reform, one that could mold and reshape "Native" habits and customs once it had been imposed on the local population. "Britons were quite open in their efforts to impose their values on local domestic arrangements," write John and Jean Comaroff in their study of colonial Africa, "and they never doubted that buildings embodied particular moral principles of conjugality and kinship" (Comaroff and Comaroff 1992: 280).

The architecture of the home was a crucial component of the discourse on domesticity. Throughout the nineteenth and early twentieth centuries, architectural writers produced model guides to domestic design geared towards a general readership. Architectural historian Gwendolyn Wright writes that "descriptions of model domestic settings supplemented the familiar florid tales of the ideal or the wayward family, providing intricate drawings and practical advice about the dwellings themselves" (Wright 1980: 9). A parallel genre grew up in Europe's colonies during the same period of time, reminding their readers that a properly ordered home was not only a source of familial pleasure but a necessary component of rule: "We do not wish to advocate an unholy haughtiness," wrote Flora Annie Steel in her 1888 book, *The Complete Indian Housekeeper and Cook*, "but an Indian household can no more be governed peacefully, without dignity and prestige, than an Indian Empire" (Steel 1888: 11). The transplanted European in their colonial domicile, through an industrious application of effort, could realize the ideals of cleanliness and order required to both run an empire effectively and insure domestic tranquility.

The bourgeois ideal of domestic comfort was seldom fully realized in the ordinary colonial domicile, however. In colonial India, evidence suggests that the colonial home was both a familiar and strange place to its occupants; a source of both homely comfort and disquieting anxiety. If the English home in colonial India provided a setting for the cultivation of habits and dispositions that authorized colonial rule, then the same structure often gave presence to a kind of "Indian-ness" that was a source of discomfort to their European occupants. What tied these two opposed senses of home life together—homely comfort and disquieting anxiety—was the architecture of the colonial domicile itself, a material and social artifact with distinctive qualities. Rather than simply symbolizing an idea of European power and authority, the colonial domicile was a complicated milieu where the attitudes and practices of European authority met with—and never fully overcame—a range of stubborn obstacles.

OCCUPYING COLONIAL HOUSES

While the phenomena I discuss below were common throughout northern India, most of the evidence presented here is drawn from the city of Lahore, the capital city of Punjab Province in British India (1849–1947).[2] By the late nineteenth century, Lahore was a desirable posting for European officers and civilians due to its large size, moderate climate, and relatively cosmopolitan range of institutions and activities. Although the European community in Lahore never exceeded a few hundred people at any time during the nineteenth century, the city's European residential district was considerably larger in area than the entire older "City" of Lahore, a mostly-Indian district that housed more than 150,000 people at the turn of the twentieth century (Figure 1). A survey conducted during the 1911 Census found that houses in Lahore's Civil Station (where European residences predominated) occupied lots averaging 2.25 acres in area; the corresponding figure for Lahore City was 0.027 acres, or roughly 1% of the Civil Station average (*Census of India* 1911: 29). The spacious lots in Lahore's Civil Station thus formed a landscape that was as conspicuous for the lavish consumption of space as it was for the presence of Europeans.

In Lahore's Civil Station, the most common type of European residence was a bungalow, a detached single-story house surrounded by a large compound that was fenced or enclosed within walls (Figure 2). Urban sociologist Anthony King has traced the evolution of the bungalow as a house type from its likely origins in Bengal province, where the term "bangla" denoted a temporary thatched structure used for residence or storage, usually in an agricultural setting. Over time, both the meaning and physical attributes of the bungalow changed, and during the colonial period the term was increasingly used in India to designate a residential structure used primarily by Europeans (King 1984).

A small minority of Europeans lived in other types of accommodation in Lahore, including residential hotels. Residential hotels became popular by the early twentieth century once "permanent or quasi-permanent residents of the station . . . acquired the *hotel habit*" (Goulding 1924: 74). But residential hotels were popular in part because they served well as temporary quarters for incoming residents while they waited for a bungalow to be vacated. In 1897, Lady Maynard, the American wife of long-time Indian civil service officer John Maynard, wrote home to her mother in Virginia from her temporary quarters in Lahore's Charing Cross hotel:

> In the February *Review of Reviews* there is an interesting article on Rudyard Kipling [who lived and worked for several years in Lahore] which I presume some of the family must have read. The engraving of the Kipling bungalow gives you a most accurate idea of an Indian bungalow (Figure 3). Everything in Lahore is built on this plan; even this hotel is exactly like it, only it has two long wings which project from either side (OIOC MSS Eur F 224/12: n.p.).

The hotel described by Lady Maynard shared another feature with the bungalow she was soon to occupy, in that both would be rented quarters. Since most colonial officers moved every few years, housing for the European community was almost always rented; in the case of government officers, the resident paid rent from his or her monthly salary earmarked as a housing allowance.

Some bungalows, especially those located in military cantonments, were built by the colonial government for its officers and employees, and standard plans were produced by the Public Works Department (PWD) for the purpose.[3] In larger cities, however, bungalows were often built by Indian businessmen and landowners who rented them both to government officers and to European civilians. Within Lahore's Civil Station (outside the military cantonment at Mian Mir), the latter was usually the case, and building permit applications housed in the Lahore Municipal Corporation record room reflect a preponderance of Indian owners over Europeans on applications for the construction of new bungalows at the turn of the century.

Reasons for the predominance of Indian owners over Europeans were multiple. For one thing, Indian proprietors often owned the building plot outright, and could therefore build without the added costs of acquiring land. For another, Indian businessmen were often willing to accept lower returns on their invested capital than European businessmen. In towns across Punjab that served as District headquarters, it was common practice for the District Commissioner, District Superintendent of Police, and Civil Surgeon (the top three government officials in District towns) to rent housing from wealthy Indian landlords, since it usually made economic sense to do so. An official in Punjab's Civil Secretariat wrote the following in 1896:

> We know that in most Punjab Stations outside Lahore the DC [District Commissioner] can usually secure an excellent house for Rs. 80/mensem . . . Native landlords are only too glad to receive as little as 3% return on capital invested in house property. Were a house of this class purchased or built by Government the rental under existing rules would probably be not less than Rs. 250/mensem, a sum altogether beyond the means of a DC, who would naturally not be prepared to

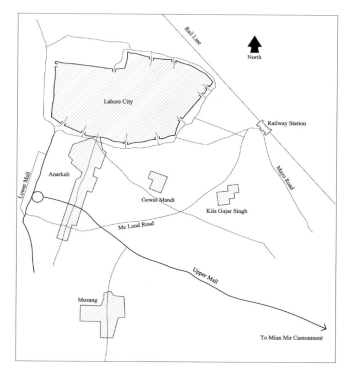

Figure 2
"Our House in Lahore, India."
Photograph c. 1890 of the
Robinson bungalow. E. Kay
Robinson was the editor of
Lahore's *Civil and Military
Gazette Press*. Rudyard
Kipling was Robinson's
assistant on the newspaper.
Source: The British Library,
Oriental and India Office
Collection. Photo 291(18), by
permission of The British
Library.

Figure 1
Lahore, c. 1900. The Civil
Station lies to the south of the
older walled district, "Lahore
City." Shaded areas
represent Indian
neighborhoods within the
municipality of Lahore.
Drawing by author.

Figure 3
Architect unknown. Rendering
of Rudyard Kipling's
Bungalow in Lahore, c. 1897
(destroyed). Source: *Review
of Reviews*, February 1897.

pay more than the customary sum (PPAP Home Department Proceedings (General) 1896/25: 28).

The temporary nature of residence, thus, and the problems this produced, was a product of colonial political economy, British administrative practices, and the control exercised over European residents by their Indian landlords. All of these features gave rise to a number of awkward problems for those who would conceive the home as a space for reflecting and helping instill in its occupants the outward marks of decorum and refinement that helped distinguish status between ruler and ruled.

TASTE, MORAL CHARACTER, AND THE BUNGALOW

The home was a critical site for cultivating the distancing postures, refinement in taste, and bourgeois moralities that underwrote inter- and intra-racial relations in the colonial city. That taste and moral character could be conceptually linked through the medium of domestic architecture is a well-established theme in studies of nineteenth-century British social history (Davidoff and Hall 1987; Girouard 1971; Marcus 1999; Markus 1982; McCleod 1971; Poovey 1995; Thompson 1988;). The works of John Claudius Loudon, who wrote treatises on gardening and architecture in the early-nineteenth century, were among the first that codified the relationship between moral character and domestic design (Loudon 1853 [1833]). For Loudon, the relationship between the two was direct:

> The perception of beauty and deformity, of refinement and grossness, of decency and vulgarity, of propriety and indecorum, is the first thing which influences man to attempt an escape from a groveling, brutish character . . . in most persons, this perception is awakened by what may be called the *exterior* of society, particularly by the mode of building. Uncouth, mean, ragged, dirty houses, constituting the body of any town, will regularly be accompanied by coarse, groveling manners. The dress, the furniture, the equipage, the mode of living, and the manners, will all correspond with the appearance of the buildings (Loudon 1953 [1833]: 3).

Schools of design were established in Britain beginning in the 1840s in an effort to elevate the standards of "taste" of the urban working classes—whose morals were deemed most in need of improvement—by training them to appreciate good design in home furnishings, tableware, and other arts of home decoration (Schmiechen 1988). Architects at home and abroad discussed the social and moral benefits of surrounding oneself with articles of daily use that exhibited qualities of polish, refinement, and good finish, each of which, in turn, helped prepare tastes, sensibilities, and personal habits that reflected the same qualities in their owners. An English commentator in an 1873 London trade journal argued that such mundane objects may indeed be more influential than the monumental designs of architects:

> There can be no doubt that altogether, independently of direct intellectual culture, either from books or society, the mind is molded and colored to a great extent by the persistent impressions produced upon it by the most familiar objects that daily meet the eye . . . and though the cathedral may produce an immense impression on a crowd, and even for the time on the human minds composing it, it will often happen that a comparatively utterly insignificant article in the house really does more in the way of impressing, or even molding, the human intelligence with which it is in almost persistent contact (cited in Grier 1997: 7).

All of this was, of course, predicated on one's ability to control basic features of the home space itself, something that was sharply limited in the colonial setting by the continual shifting of residences and reliance upon previous tenants—or the whims of a Native landlord—for keeping the house in good repair. F. S. Growse, a self-described "apostle of culture," trenchant critic of the Public Works Department, colonial government servant, and amateur architect of some note, records in his memoir (1886) having actually turned down a transfer to another station in India simply because the house he would occupy left "no scope for the exercise of individual taste."

> I declined [the transfer] solely on account of the house there, though it had been built by no less distinguished a character than Mr. A. O. Hume, and at enormous cost to the owner . . . [It was] an impossibility to put up pictures or hangings, or to give the interior anything of a home-like appearance, and I therefore—on this account alone—declined the transfer. A plain, roomy, weather-tight barn would have suited me far better (Growse 1886: v).

Being more or less constantly on the move meant that whatever one possessed by way of "household decoration" had to be relatively mobile, disposable, or not liable to be missed when left behind. Furnishings of the proper sort were scarce in most cities, and most were acquired "on the cheap" at moving sales, or at sales accompanying European funerals in the city. A genre of "ladies" periodical literature and household decoration guides grew up to address the need for cheap furnishings and economical decoration ideas by the latter half of the nineteenth century, and the classified section of English newspapers in Lahore, as elsewhere, regularly advertised furnishings for sale (Figure 4).[4]

Figure 4
Page from *Mackenzie, Lyall and Company* auction catalog in Calcutta, 1851. Notice the entry for "neat household furniture" at the bottom of the page. Source: Colesworthy Grant 1984 [1862], p. 38.

Keeping a proper home, with its requisite furnishings and appliances, was one way of making the bungalow an "island of Englishness," in the words of Thomas Metcalf—a social and architectural setting which distanced itself from the promiscuous and degraded context of the Indian city as European residents perceived it (Metcalf 1994: 178). Even within the White community, however, differences in status were open to view, and the bungalow was an important site of social anchorage for marking and maintaining those differences. Esmee Mascall's memoir of growing up in Lahore in the early twentieth century illustrates how basic social rituals that Europeans were familiar with from home, once adapted to a range of different material and social circumstances in the colony, threw status negotiations between Europeans into new kinds of relationships. "I must describe the dinner-party of those days," Mascall wrote, "because one saw nothing quite like it in England."

> Table servants of the invited guest would turn up to help wait at table, bringing with them, very likely, anything in the way of silver and cutlery of which the host might be in short supply for a dinner of seven courses and ten or twelve table guests. Nothing was said about this beforehand, but when the host saw unfamiliar items on his table—and these of course were recognized by one or other of his guests—it was *just an amusing joke*, and the guest's servant saw to it that all the borrowed items went back safely (OIOC MSS Eur C 427: 27).

Mascall's dissembling comment that a shortage of cutlery "was just an amusing joke" highlights, of course, the social impropriety that situation might present in England. Such, too, was the case with creating a proper setting for polite dining, one that would reflect on the skills of an English hostess in telling ways:

> If you had a new *khitmatgar* [parlourman] who had perhaps been in service with a bachelor, you might find rather a dreadful decoration on the table in place of the English-style silver vases with flowers . . . one had to be tactful and warn the man well beforehand that vases of flowers were the right thing for the English Sahib's table (OIOC MSS Eur C 427: 29).

Another memoir written by a British woman resident in Lahore (c. 1915) relates an incident in which similarly mundane features of the house were drawn subtly into a commentary on distinction: "The baths [in our bungalow] were made of tin and filled with boiling water from old kerosene tins," the author wrote.

> It did not even seem strange when my father, as an act of devotion to my mother, imported an English porcelain bath which was filled with the kerosene tins as before. A number of ladies came to refresh their memories and admire this object in its alien setting. An Indian friend who had not seen such a thing before gazed for some time and finally remarked, "he must love you very much" (OIOC MSS Eur D 1197: n.p.).

THE CONSTRUCTION OF BUNGALOWS

In addition to matters of taste in furnishing and decoration—both constrained by the peripatetic nature of English residence in the city—the architectural quality of the bungalow itself often worked against British efforts to establish the right kind of domestic milieu. Consider the predicament of Martyn, a protagonist in Rudyard Kipling's short story "William the Conqueror" (c. 1890). The building Kipling described was no doubt similar to many he would have known from his years living in Lahore, and the story from which this excerpt is taken is set in that city.

> As an Acting District Superintendent of Police, Martyn drew the mag-
> nificent pay of six hundred depreciated silver rupees a month and his
> little four-roomed bungalow said just as much. There were the usual
> blue-and-white striped jail-made rugs on the uneven floor; the usual
> glass-studded Amritsar *phulkaris* [embroidered cloth] draped to nails
> driven into the flaking whitewash of the walls; the usual half-dozen
> chairs that did not match, picked up at sales of dead men's effects;
> and the usual streaks of black grease where the leather *punkah*-thong
> [*punkah*=fan] ran through the wall. It was as though everything had been
> unpacked the night before to be repacked next morning . . . Thus did
> people live who had such an income; and in a land where each man's
> pay, age, and position are printed in a book, that all may read, it is hardly
> worthwhile to play at pretenses in word or deed (Kipling cited in
> Maugham 1952: 205).

Furnishings and architectural features of the bungalow are prominent in this
story, and they reinforce Kipling's emphasis on Martyn's lowly status. Kipling
suggests that maintaining an air of civility in a house whose architectural features constantly mitigated against it was an ongoing battle for those "who had
such an income." There is ample evidence to suggest, however, that people like
Martyn shared their predicament with residents of much higher standing. Even
relatively fine bungalows were often poorly planned, simply appointed, and difficult to maintain.

In 1910, the Crown Prince of Germany visited India and stayed in a government bungalow near Delhi, by then Punjab's largest city. In anticipation of the
Prince's visit, Major E. Wilkinson, the province's sanitary commissioner, conducted a walk-through tour of the bungalow in order to certify its suitability for
the visiting dignitary and his entourage of more than seventy people. Wilkinson's
detailed notes from the tour provide a glimpse into the kind of housing meant
to be, quite literally, fit for a prince at the time.

> Ventilation [in the house] is imperfect, the windows not having been
> well arranged . . . The bathrooms have linoleum over a rough stone floor
> (rather than glazed tiles) and the walls (as also those of some of the
> other rooms) are whitewashed rather than painted. Some of the baths
> are provided with long enameled tubs, others with ordinary galvanized
> tubs, and although all have water taps, these are for cold water only . . .
> There are only ordinary, dry pattern, commodes instead of water clos-
> ets [in the bathrooms]. The waste water of bathrooms, etc. is discharged
> into sumps just outside the buildings from which it has to be dipped . . .
> The kitchen is small and dirty. It is only provided with ordinary *chulas*
> [open stoves] for charcoal. There is only one water tap and there is no
> proper sink for washing cooking vessels, etc. There is a small sink in
> the floor below the tap, but this is quite unsuitable (PPAP Home De-
> partment Proceedings [Medical and Sanitary] 1910/242: n.p.).

Wilkinson ordered a number of remedial improvements to be made, including constructing underground drainage pipes to carry away waste-water, placing a sink and range in the kitchen, and adding tiles to the kitchen and bathroom
walls. If these types of deficiencies could be remedied, on occasion, others could
not be. Foremost among these, perhaps, was the decidedly "Indian" look of the
basic architectural details that gave the bungalow its character—including those
commented upon by Kipling—since the materials and manner of construction
of bungalows helped assimilate them visually to an architectural landscape that
was common and local.

With few exceptions, the structure and finish of bungalows were exactly like
those of Indian residential buildings in other parts of the city, even if the style
and layout of bungalows and the social uses they accommodated were mark-
edly different. The labor of building a bungalow was done almost exclusively by
Indian craftsmen, usually organized by Indian contractors. Many bungalows,

indeed, were designed by Indian architects, who nevertheless worked according to English tastes and specifications. Each of the building trades involved in bungalow construction—excavation, masonry, carpentry, and tile work—were ones whose customary techniques and materials had long been in use in northern India, and the personnel involved in construction learned their specialization through apprenticeships in guilds whose rights to membership were hereditary.[5] Although changes in construction practice were introduced during the colonial period—including the gradual substitution of engineered standards for rules of thumb in the sizing of structural members, new methods of iron construction adopted from European practice, and the use of glazed windows in place of grilled or shuttered openings—the tangible qualities of a bungalow's physical fabric remained rooted in Indian, not English, architectural traditions (Figure 5).

Material alterations over time to the original Bengali dwelling included the substitution of brick and other materials for thatch, changes in the "size, number and arrangement of rooms," and the adoption of a range of domestic equipment and mechanical devices not commonly found in the Indian prototype (King 1984: 51). By the late -nineteenth century in Lahore, as elsewhere, the bungalow was highly standardized with regard to room arrangement, mode of construction, and overall appearance.

Like houses in the Indian quarters of the city, the majority of Lahore's bungalows had flat roofs covered with clay tiles or lime plaster. The roof's outer surface was built up over a thin layer of compressed earth, which was in turn underlain by masonry tiles. Wooden "battens" three- to four-inches wide and from six- to eight-inches deep were used as ceiling and floor joists, spaced roughly one foot apart. Where battens met the brick supporting walls of the house, a receiving pocket was made by leaving a brick out. Joists were made from *deodar* if possible, a species of cedar known for its resistance to white ants and rot, and they rested in turn on intermittent wooden or iron beams, sized according to their material strength and span (Figure 6).

Similarly, like all other buildings in Lahore, the bungalow's supporting walls, foundations, and interior partitions were all built of bricks, most produced locally in the numerous kilns that encircled the city. Throughout the city, Lahore's distinctive brick architecture predominated, leading one traveler to comment that, in Lahore:

> *Everything* is brick; confounded brick, walls, houses, pagodas, temples of any and every description, confounded brick. Go where you will, the bricks still stick to you. Up this street, with its wretched pavement of loose stones, and down that with its tottering old dwellings made since the day of Adam, there is nothing but brick (OIOC Mss Eur B 366: n.p.).

English standard brick sizes ($2^1/4$ inches by $3^5/8$ inches by $7^5/8$ inches) were introduced into Punjab province around the 1880s, but local bricks with their distinctive shapes were used for construction well into the twentieth century. Walls made from the latter were built unnecessarily thick from a structural standpoint, a technique that eliminated the need for formal structural calculations, just as it insulated the interior spaces of the house well from the Punjab's punishing sun. Kiln-fired bricks were set in lime mortar in a well-built structure, and lime was produced locally from *kankar*—calcitic nodules found at shallow depths in the soil around Lahore. On less expensive buildings, sun-dried bricks were set in mud plaster.

The materials used on the exterior of the bungalow, too, were identical to those used on Indian houses. The usual treatment was to cover the exterior walls in lime plaster and paint or whitewash them a light color. Alternately, the walls could be finished with *surkhi*, a reddish plaster made from pulverized bricks. On buildings plastered with *surkhi*, mortar lines were sometimes inscribed into the finish coat to replicate the appearance of unplastered English bricks, thereby lending an air of decorative refinement to what was otherwise a common local idiom. Other decorative features were added to the bungalow's exterior that

Figure 5
Eighteenth- and nineteenth-century domestic architecture in a suburb of Lahore. Notice the predominance of plastered brick enclosing walls. The small building in the foreground is an older pleasure pavilion now occupied as a dwelling. Photo by author.

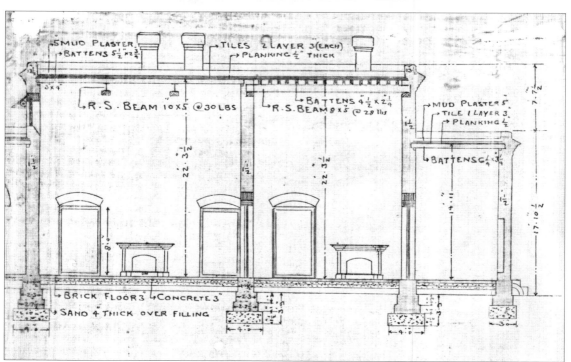

Figure 6
Architect unknown. Bungalow on Lytton road, cross-section, 1907. Dimensions are given in feet and inches. Source: Municipal Corporation of Lahore.

reflected European styles common in the nineteenth century, including neoclassical and gothic revival versions. Notably, this was a practice increasingly adopted by architects of Indian houses in the city by the end of the nineteenth century as well (Figure 7).

Applied stylistic features aside, thus, the mundane features of bungalow construction served to distance them from the "small, cozy" English houses Nawab Mehdi Hasan Khan described above as being "the kind of abode[s] in which our retired Lieutenant Governors live." These kinds of differences are important, as historian Dell Upton has argued, since conventions of construction help establish "a context or system of common understanding" within which visual clues to meaning become more or less obvious, a system in which "allusions suffice" (Upton 1977: 102). In the colonial context, a distinctly different system of building conventions from those present in England lent an air of strangeness to European homes in India that was often commented upon: "The exterior of the bungalow will, I doubt not, be sufficient to impress you with a feeling of *absence from old England*," wrote Colesworthy Grant, in his 1862 guide to Anglo-Indian domestic life; "that it is 'no your ain [own] house, you'll 'ken [know] by the rigging o't" (Grant 1984 [1862]: 8).

Figure 7
Neoclassical and other ornamental details on an Indian residence in the suburb of Anarkali, Lahore, c. 1900. Notice the rusticated base, corinthian pilaster capitals, and classical molding at the roof cornice; these features coexist with brackets, wooden balconies, and a central bay window decorated with traditional Indian motifs. Photo by author.

British writers also regularly complained that buildings constructed by Indians were inadequately built and sloppily finished, something that made the bungalow seem further distant from English ideals of decorum and refinement—qualities the home was supposed to both reflect and help produce in its occupants.

> All the work that I have seen turned out by Native hands is bad. Doors don't come up properly to the jambs; windows are never straight; there is no finish in the roofs. Floors and plinths are badly put down, and timber is wastefully misused without any increase in strength. Native hinges and locks, and ironwork more generally, are all abominations to English eyes. There is no correct rabbeting, mortising, mitering, dovetailing or joinery of any sort in the land—as far as I have seen; and this disgusts me a good deal . . . The Anglo-Indians have a beautifully expressive word for all this—"*kutcha*." Everything is "*kutcha*"—which means everything is just as an English workman would not turn it out (Kipling cited in Pinney 1986: 188).[6]

If the bungalow was, in part, a setting for the cultivation and display of refined manners and taste, then its physical appearance played a role in the pervasive sense of anxiety about the effects on human character of living in a colony highlighted in European writings. The bungalow's walls, rooms, doors, and furnishings became a focus of comparison between qualities found in English and Indian homes, just as they served as vexing reminders of the co-presence of different sensory qualities, meanings, and values tied to more local histories of production and use (Serematakis 1994: 136).

THE SOCIAL ORGANIZATION OF DOMESTIC SPACE

More than material qualities played a role in making bungalows seem inadequate to their purposes, however. The social functions these houses had to accommodate required an orchestrated arrangement of spaces that was difficult to manage in a bungalow. The bungalow's relatively simple layout served a variety of social purposes. Most bungalows were built near the center of an enclosed plot of sufficient area to insure a free flow of breeze across it. Servants' quarters, animal, vehicle, and other kinds of storage sheds were arrayed along one edge of the plot out of view from the main rooms of the house, and a separate structure placed closer to the main dwelling was used for the kitchen (Figure 8). In plan, the rooms of the main dwelling were almost always arranged with bi-axial symmetry. Each corner of the roughly square building contained a rectangular room with smaller auxiliary spaces attached to it (used for bathing and dressing when the room was a bedroom). The corner rooms along one side of the bungalow either shared a common wall, or shared walls with a third, intervening room, and were separated from the attached rooms on the other side by a central hall which could be divided into two or more separate spaces. The rooms of the central hall were used for dining and entertaining guests (Figure 9).

Despite the bungalow's strict symmetry, the central hall intersected with the outer walls at two opposite ends, forming the "front" of the structure on one side and the "back" at the other. Ceilings in the central hall were usually taller than those over the suite of rooms on either side to facilitate ventilation in the center of the house. In a humbler structure, the central hall could be omitted altogether, leaving a four-square plan which retained, nevertheless, the front/back distinction (Figure 10). A projecting porch sometimes marked the front façade of the bungalow and served as a covered entryway. In most cases, a broad verandah surrounded the bungalow on three or four sides, and the whole composition was raised several feet above the ground on a masonry plinth. Large and more elaborate bungalows meant for senior government officers existed in Lahore, as in other large towns and cities, and the specialized rooms in these buildings could exceed in number those described above. However, the majority of British residents' houses in Lahore were of the type just described.

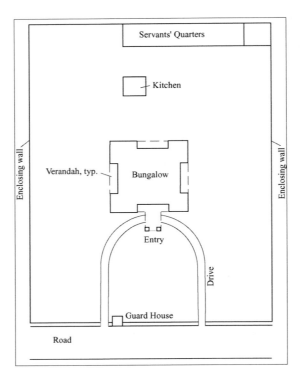

Figure 8
Typical site plan of
a bungalow in its
compound. Drawing
by author.

Figure 9
Architect unknown. Bungalow
on Beadon road, Lahore, plan
and section, 1887. Source:
Municipal Corporation of
Lahore.

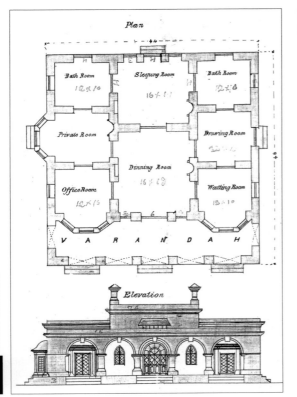

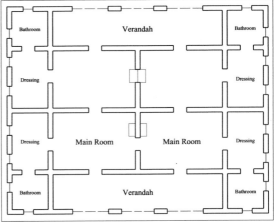

Figure 10
Four-square bungalow, plan,
typical, Drawing by author
based on plan by Kanhayalal,
Executive Engineer, Shahpur
District, 1902. In simpler four-
square plans, the dressing
rooms and bathrooms would
be omitted.

The "front" and "back" of the bungalow established an imaginary axis that divided more public functions in the house from those which were considered to be more private. In this way, the vertical segregation of activity described above by Nawab Mehdi Hasan Khan for a typical London row-house was accomplished, in the bungalow, horizontally. Rooms at the front of the house were used for entertaining visitors or overnight guests, and in the case of a government officer's residence, at least one room was required to be set aside as a place for meeting the area's residents on matters concerning local governance. The presence of an office in the bungalow meant that residence and office functions coexisted in the same structure, adding a further layer of complexity to the building's program of use.

The nineteenth-century European bourgeois ideal of proper domestic arrangements specified clear separations between less- and more-private spaces in the house, between servants and family members, and between people of different sexes and ages. The house plan ideally segregated different activities from one another and provided a separate space for each.

> It is a first principle with the better classes of English people that the Family Rooms shall be essentially private, and as much as possible the Family Thoroughfares [hallways]. It becomes the foremost of all maxims, therefore, however small the establishment, that the Servants' Department shall be separated from the Main House, so that what passes on either side of the boundary shall be both invisible and inaudible on the other . . . In short, whether in a small house or a large one, let the family have free passage without encountering the servants unexpectedly, and let the servants have access to all their duties without coming unexpectedly upon the family or visitors (Kerr 1864: 74–5).

These kinds of separations were an important condition for maintaining a code of personal demeanor, called "gentility" in the nineteenth century, necessary to illicit respect: "A respectable person imagined [herself] as the occupant of a discrete envelope of social and physical space within which . . . she was entitled to remain undisturbed in return for respecting the integrity of others' boundaries" (Upton 1998: 158). Bungalows were organized to serve these needs too, but the relations of domestic labor they were supported by, along with the physical distribution of spaces they housed, constantly worked against the ideal.

One of the key points of conflict was, of course, the disposition of household servants.[7] Even a relatively modest European household in India would maintain several specialized servants to conduct most of the daily labor of the house, from cooking, gardening, and cleaning out the house's rooms, to serving as wet-nurses and *ayahs* (nannies) for European infants and children (Figure 11). The co-presence of Indian servants in the innermost recesses of the home was thought to expose its occupants to a range of social (and physical) dangers that derived, in part, from fears of racial mixing. As Ann Laura Stoler has argued, "middle-class colonials . . . embodied a set of fundamental tensions between a culture of whiteness that cordoned itself off from the native world and a set of domestic arrangements and class distinctions among Europeans that produced cultural hybridities and sympathies that repeatedly transgressed these distinctions" (Stoler 1995: 112). These tensions included the possibility that European children would develop overly affective ties to their Indian *ayahs* and acquire bad habits of personality—or even take on their pernicious racial traits through the medium of wet nurses' milk; the fear of servants' sexual profligacy or of their becoming a source of sexual arousal for their colonial masters; and the threat that letting down one's guard over personal demeanor might incite insurrection or ridicule, either of which could dismantle the social distance that justified colonial rule itself.[8]

The layout of bungalows mediated these threats imperfectly, since one of their key qualities was porosity between the interior rooms of the house and the house's exterior. Inside the house, the desire for ventilation argued against

Figure 11
"Ayah." Illustration from Colesworthy Grant's book, *Anglo–Indian Domestic Life*. Grant writes, "the services of a native nurse [ayah] is but an exchange, after all, of corporeal for mental trouble on the part of parents who are solicitous about their children's minds, and anxious to check the growth of dangerous habits and unamiable traits of character which are too often, and imperceptibly contracted during their association with the native servant." Source: Grant 1984 [1862], 112.

the use of interior hallways that could separate and channel the flow of activity from one space to the next. The less-private rooms of the house opened directly onto more private ones, therefore, without the intervening buffer provided by a hallway. Opening the interior rooms of the house to cooling breezes during the summer was indeed one of the critical design criteria for bungalows. The encircling verandah was an important feature of the design for this purpose, since it cooled air in immediate proximity to the house and provided an open but covered space for use in the evenings and at other times during cooler months of the year. Verandahs also served many of the functions of an interior hallway since most rooms of the house opened onto them directly through doorways, or at least visually through windows. But verandahs were also spaces for conducting a range of household labor tasks, and servants often slept there at night or took rest in their shade during the day. This weakened their usefulness as a separating device, and provided obvious opportunities for spatial transgression (Figure 12).

Figure 12
Schematic plan of a bungalow showing points of entry into household rooms directly from the verandah. Drawing by author.

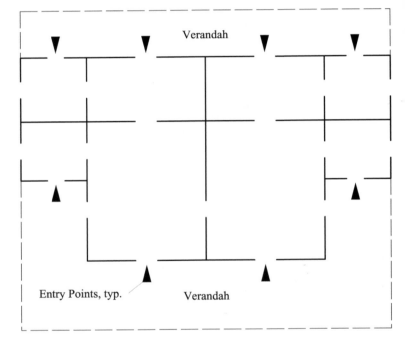

The uncanny associations provoked by the almost continual presence of servants in and around the bungalow, and the difficulty of policing their movements, formed a regular theme in Rudyard Kipling's literature. In his short story, "The House of Shadows" (1887), Kipling suggested the sense of anxiety these conditions could lead to. Here, as elsewhere, Kipling used a popular late-nineteenth-century literary device, the "haunted house" story, to evoke a common sentiment.[9] The following passage merits quoting at length:

> My grievance, so far as I can explain it in writing, is that there are far too many tenants in the eight, lime-washed rooms for which I pay seventy five rupees a month . . . At breakfast, in the full fresh daylight, I am conscious that some one who is not the *khitmatgar* is watching the back of my head from the door that leads into my bedroom; when I turn sharply, the *purday* [curtain] is dropped and I only see it waving gently as though shaken by the wind . . . I would endure the people who hide in the corners of the lamproom and rush out when my back is turned,

the persons who get between the *almirah* and the wall when I come into my dressing-room hastily at dusk, or even the person in the garden who slides in and out of the *ferash* trees when I walk there, if I could only get rid of the *Man in the Next room*. There is no sense in him, and he interferes sadly with one's work. I believe now that if he dared he would come out from the other side of the *purday* and peep over my shoulder to see what I am writing. But he is afraid and is now twitching the cord that works the ventilating window . . . You will concede, will you not, that this is annoying, particularly when I know that I am officially the sole tenant. No man, visible or invisible, has a right to spy upon my outgoings or incomings (Kipling cited in Pinney 1986: 246–8).

As in the quote from Kipling's story about Martyn earlier, physical features of the bungalow are prominent in this passage. The Anglo-Indian nomenclature used for these features along with the emotional content Kipling evokes in the story work in unison to characterize a peculiarly colonial form of unhomely discomfort. In the end, Kipling's narrator abandons the bungalow for a revivifying spell at a "hill-station."[10] While this was a remedy many Europeans could and did resort to in India, more immediate approaches to the same problems were required. Foremost among these was a search for methods of governing conduct in the colonial household; a task both announced by and facilitated through the publication of guides to household management published from the mid-nineteenth century onwards in India.

SETTING THE HOUSEHOLD RIGHT

A perusal of colonial household manuals collected in the British Library reveals their ubiquity during the late nineteenth century. The Anglo-Indian household manual is a strange kind of hybrid text. Part nineteenth-century "book of manners," part domestic science, and part colonial folk ethnography, the household manual is largely focused on techniques for managing Indian servants and converting unfamiliar settings and foods into a reasonable facsimile of their English equivalents. The social environment of the English residence, adapted to conditions of life in a colonial setting, was likened to a microcosm of empire in these works, and their announced task, under the circumstances, was to provide a guide for establishing parallel qualities between the two. "Here, as there [in England], the end and object is not merely personal comfort, but the formation of a home," wrote Flora Annie Steel, "that unit of civilization where father and children, master and servant, employer and employed, can learn their several duties" (Steel 1888: 7).

Mirroring in miniature the ordering of imperial relations more generally, order in the colonial home depended in part upon classificatory schemes that divided servants according to race, religion, and gender. In *Anglo-Indian Domestic Life* (1862), a text of immeasurable value to the historian of that subject, Colesworthy Grant devoted several pages to a hierarchically ranked list of all the domestic servants found in a colonial home. Each type of servant was described according to his or her race and social standing in Indian society more generally, along with the problems and benefits of service according to each. Steel wrote that, in her guide, "an attempt has been made to assimilate the duties of each servant to those of his or her English compeer, and thus to show the new-comer where fault lies" (Steel 1888: vi).

Given the above, the idea that these manuals are best read as bulwarks of Foucauldian disciplinarity is common in the secondary literature, and not without some justification.[11] Nevertheless, they also reveal evidence of a matrix of overlapping disciplines in the bungalow, one that juxtaposed different spatial practices—Indian and English—each with its own sets of demands and criteria of competence. Saying this is to suggest that particular spaces, material environments, and assemblages of sensory media may themselves embed memories and particular "ways of inhabiting" for those properly prepared to receive them. The spatial practices engaged in by servants around the bungalow are rendered quite thinly in these manuals as the products of "custom" or "habit"—in short, as time-worn cultural predilections. But they emerge clearly, nevertheless, as a primary object of concern, and one for which a range of techniques is suggested in order to root them out.

"Pay periodic visits of inspection to [the servants'] quarters," wrote the author of a 1906 manual, "to see that a few obvious sanitary rules are not neglected" (Calvert 1906: 5). The same author argued that such inspections were best conducted on the Sabbath, for reasons that did not need elaboration. Steel (1888) wrote that, "it is as well . . . to eat your breakfast in peace before venturing into the pantry and cook-room" (p. 10); but do so nevertheless, she suggested, lest the mistress of the house discover "the khitmatgar using his toes as an efficient toast-rack" (p. 2).

Indeed, an underlying theme of these works is that of the Indian servant occupying the colonial domicile with a far greater degree of comfort than their colonial masters. Vigilance has to be maintained, Steel wrote, to keep servants from "turning your domain into a caravanserai for their relations to the third and fourth generation" (Steel 1888: 4). In another passage, she warned that "few mistresses have been long in India without having had the trouble of scandals between the ayah and the other servants" (Steel 1888: 67). The kitchen, servants' quarters, pantry, and stables are all singled out as "native" spaces in these works, suggesting that more than one mode of sociality, and more than one domestic sensorium, cohabited the bungalow compound.

CONCLUSION

The history of colonial urbanism has often been written as the incomplete imposition of Western forms of society, politics, and technology in a non-Western setting (Evenson, 1989; Kennedy 1996b; King 1976, 1991; Tillotson 1989). The role of built form in this history is usually to serve as a backdrop for the telling of events or else to provide incontrovertible material evidence of the intentions of a foreign ruling elite. As this article has shown, however, a study of the intentions that lay behind the way colonial buildings were constructed, inhabited, and socially organized is never wholly adequate for conducting a history of their use and meaning.

Prior scholarship has emphasized British debates during the late nineteenth and early twentieth centuries about the style of architecture most suited to Britain's exalted place in the colonial order, debates that clearly illustrate elite intentions (Baucom 1999; Crinson, 1996; Metcalf 1989; Tillotson 1989). The resolution of those debates can be readily seen in the Victoria Stations, Government Houses, and High Court buildings that stand out so strikingly in India's landscape. These buildings were clearly designed to "impress" a colonized audience through their scale and grandeur, and through the symbolic content of their ornament. Even monumental architecture is never simply inertly symbolic, however. If "England's architectures" were sometimes transported to the colony, as Ian Baucom has argued, they were also always open to reinterpretation, misunderstanding, and the transformation of meaning through use. "As [colonial] subjects took their places" in these settings, Baucom writes, "they also took partial possession of those places, estranging them, and, in the process, transforming the narratives of English identity that these spaces promised to locate" (Baucom 1999: 38).

There is great need to rethink the grand monuments of empire with a closer attention to their materiality and transformation through use. Such studies would certainly challenge the idea that colonial power flowed unchecked in its drive to dominate local cultures. But the grounding of colonial power depended as much on everyday and small-scale practices as it did on the display of monumental buildings or public rituals of statecraft. Indeed, in the colonial context, as Ann Laura Stoler has argued, it was "the domestic domain, not the public sphere, where [the] essential dispositions of manliness, bourgeois morality, and racial attribute could be dangerously undone or securely made" (Stoler 1995: 108). Always imperfect for the task, the bungalow nevertheless formed an important setting for enacting those small-scale and everyday practices. Not simply an icon of authority, the bungalow was a critical site for cultivating the habits of "self-control, self-discipline, and self-determination" required to comport the self with authority (Stoler 1995: 10). As I have shown, however, the material qualities of the bungalow's construction and the social arrangements they were meant to help constitute problematized the everyday expectations and sensory perceptions that, while matters of commonplace for the English at home were de-familiarized and brought prominently to attention in the colonial setting. If the usual trope for describing the colonial bungalow is that it "served to impress Indians with the power and authority of the British," then this is a trope more closely attuned with intention than with an actually realized set of practices.[12] Instead, as I have argued, it is more useful to think of the bungalow as a milieu for the cultivation of attitudes and behaviors necessary to evoke authority, than as a building type that evoked the same thing.

ACKNOWLEDGMENT

The author wishes to thank Ross Wienert for drafting assistance on the illustrations for this article.

NOTES

1. Nawab Mehdi Hasan Khan, Chief Justice of Hyderabad, Deccan, reprinted in *The Punjab Magazine* 233 (1890): 28, 31.
2. For a counter example of European residences in eighteenth- and nineteenth-century Calcutta, see Chattopadhyay (2000). The residences Chattopadhyay describes predate most of the buildings discussed below.
3. PWD bungalows are discussed, among other places, in Tillotson (1989). Tillotson writes, "The PWD established standard plans, so that all but the most important buildings were designed and constructed according to fixed principles, merely adapted to meet particular needs. These standard plans offered, as it were, colonial bungalows off the peg, with instructions about how they could be modified to make them serve one function or another. An order of 1864 expressly forbade any deviation from the standard plans . . . Rudyard Kipling summed up the more modest productions of the PWD more tersely with his term 'bungaloathsome'" (pp. 71–2). Also see Davies (1985); King (1984); Metcalf (1989); Morris (1986); Stamp (1981).
4. From the editor of *The Bungalow: A Paper for Anglo Indian Homes* [1896-?]: "In bringing out *The Bungalow*, the Editor hopes to supply a much-felt want—a ladies paper that will devote itself to the interests of Anglo Indian Homes. There will be every month articles on 'The Home: how to beautify it,' with many hints on decoration, by a lady who has spent many years in Indian bungalows, Indian Cookery, with Recipes and Menus, 'Lessons on Home Dressmaking,' 'Gardening,' 'The Toilet,' fashions, etc. There will also be a column of ladies private advertisement for articles for sale and exchange, and several prizes will be offered for competition each month." On the role of women in outfitting and governing the colonial domicile see Chattopadhyay (2002).
5. In the 1901 Census, 16,700 persons were listed as working in miscellaneous building trades in Punjab province; by 1911, the number had risen to over 100,000, reflecting an increase of more than 500%. Trades which showed big increases during this period included cabinet makers and carriage painters (280%), thatchers, building contractors, house painters, tilers, plumbers, locksmiths (500%), trade in dyes, paints and petroleum (200%), brick and tile makers (100%), and trade in furniture, carpets, curtains and bedding (210%). Figures calculated from tables in *Census of India, 1911*.
6. The same assessment extended to Indian furniture, cabinet, and carriage design and finish: "Native-made English carriages are, in general, clumsily and coarsely made, and, even if elegant in shape, are always found wanting in finish . . . the average *tarkhan* [carpenter] has no idea of getting a polish on his work. He thinks a couple, or at most three, coats of paint daubed on the carriage quite sufficient for all practical purposes, and he does not allow a sufficient interval between the different coats" (O'Dwyer 1889: 17).

The idea that Indian craftsmanship is substandard may continue to reso-nate in some circles within Britain. The following news item appeared in a recent *New York Times*: "Prince Philip, husband of Queen Elizabeth, said during a tour of a factory in Scotland that an unsophisticated fuse box looked 'as though it was put in by an Indian.' Racial equality groups expressed anger and Philip swiftly apologized." See "Princely Gaffe," *The New York Times* August 11 1999: A6.

7. The Indian staff of a bungalow residence were frequent subjects of "mem-oir-like" accounts by Europeans, and the portraits drawn of them were usu-ally unflattering. Perhaps the most famous work in this genre is Atkinson (1860). Atkinson's book included forty watercolor plates of domestic scenes from a bungalow, most of which lampoon and exaggerate the physical and racial characteristics of typical bungalow staff, along with their perceived lassitude.

8. Stoler (1995, Chapter 5: 146) writes "one seventeenth-century French doctor took as a given that breastmilk 'had the power to make children resemble their nurses in mind and body, just as the seed makes them resemble their mother and father.'"

9. For a succinctly sketched history of this genre as it relates to urban hous-ing see Marcus (1999), especially Chapter 3. For connections between haunted house stories and Freud's elucidation of the "uncanny" see Vidler (1992).

10. On the British hill station as a resort for Europeans, see Kennedy (1996a).

11. John and Jean Comaroff offered the following summary and qualification of this kind of argument: "If the likes of Foucault are correct [a naturalized notion of domesticity] was an element in the making of a total moral order, a silent edifice in which family and home served as mechanisms of disci-pline and social control. Vested in dispersed regimes of surveillance and in the texture of everyday habit, goes the general argument, the doctrine of domesticity facilitated new forms of production, new structures of inequal-ity. Still, we repeat, it did not prevail immediately or without resistance—nor everywhere in just the same way" (Comaroff and Comaroff 1992: 267).

12. Thomas Metcalf (1994: 177–8) writes, for example, that "the size of the compound, together with its wall, gate, guard, and long entry drive, served to impress Indians with the power and authority of the British, while at the same time affording a way of regulating entry."

REFERENCES

Atkinson, George Franklin. 1860. *Curry and Rice on Forty Plates: Or, the Ingredients of Social Life at "Our Station" in India*. London: W. Thacker and Company.

Baucom, Ian. 1999. *Out of Place: Englishness, Empire, and the Locations of Identity*. Princeton, NJ: Princeton University Press.

Calvert, J. T. 1906. *On the Preservation of Health for the Guidance of Young Officers on their Arrival in India*. Calcutta: The Bengal Secretariat Press.

Chatterjee, Partha. 1993. *The Nation and its Fragments: Colonial and Post-colonial Histories*. Princeton, NJ: Princeton University Press.

Chattopadhyay, Swati. 2000. "Blurring Boundaries: The Limits of 'White Town' in Colonial Calcutta." *Journal of the Society of Architectural Historians* 59(2): 154–79.

Chattopadhyay, Swati. 2002. "'Goods, Chattels and Sundry Items': Constructing 19th-Century Anglo-Indian Domestic Life." *Journal of Material Culture* 7(3): 243–71.

Comaroff, John and Jean Comaroff. 1992. *Ethnography and the Historical Imagination*. Boulder, CO: Westview Press.

Crinson, Mark. 1996. *Empire Building: Orientalism and Victorian Architecture*. London: Routledge.

Davidoff, Leonore and Catherine Hall. 1987. *Family Fortunes: Men and Women of the English Middle Class, 1780–1850*. Chicago, IL: University of Chicago Press.

Davies, Philip. 1985. *Splendours of the Raj: British Architecture in India, 1660 to 1947*. London: J. Murray.

Evenson, Norma. 1989. *The Indian Metropolis: A View Toward the West*. New Haven, CT: Yale University Press.

Girouard, Mark. 1971. *The Victorian Country House*. New Haven, CT: Yale University Press.

Goulding, H. R. 1924. *Old Lahore: Reminiscences of a Resident*. Lahore: Sang-e-Meel Publications.

Grant, Colesworthy. 1984 [1862]. *Anglo-Indian Domestic Life: A Letter from an Artist in India to his Mother in England*. Calcutta: Subornorekha.

Grier, Catherine. 1997. *Culture and Comfort: Parlour-Making and Middle-Class Identity, 1850–1930*. Washington, DC: Smithsonian Institution Press.

Growse, F. S. 1886. *Indian Architecture of Today: As Exemplified in New Buildings in the Bulandshahr District*. Benaras: Medical Hall Press.

Hall, Catherine. 2002. *Civilising Subjects: Metropole and Colony in the English Imagination, 1830–1867*. Oxford: Polity Press.

Kennedy, Dane. 1996a. *The Magic Mountains: Hill Stations and the British Raj*. Berkeley, CA: University of California Press.

Kennedy, Dane. 1996b. "Imperial History and post-Colonial Theory." *Journal of Imperial and Commonwealth History* 24(3): 345–63.

Kerr, Robert. 1864. *The Gentleman's House; Or, How to Plan English Residences, From the Parsonage to the Palace*. London: John Murray.

King, Anthony D. 1976. *Colonial Urban Development: Culture, Social Power and Environment*. London: Routledge and Kegan Paul.

King, Anthony D. *The Bungalow: The Production of a Global Culture*. London: Routledge and Kegan Paul.

King, Anthony D. 1991. *Urbanism, Colonialism, and the World-Economy: Cultural and Spatial Foundations of the World Urban System*. London: Routledge.

Loudon, John Claudius. 1853 [1833]. *An Encyclopedia of Cottage, Farm, and Villa Architecture and Furniture; Containing Numerous Designs for Dwellings, From the Villa to the Cottage and the Farm*, 2nd edn. London: Longman, Brown, Green, and Longmans.

Marcus, Sharon. 1999. *Apartment Stories: City and Home in Nineteenth-Century Paris and London*. Berkeley, CA: University of California Press.

Maughan, W. Somerset (ed.). 1952. *A Choice of Kipling's Prose*. London: Macmillan and Company.

Markus, Thomas. 1982. *Order in Space and Society: Architectural Form and its Context in the Scottish Enlightenment*. Edinburgh: Mainstream.

McCleod, Robert. 1971. *Style and Society: Architectural Ideology in Britain, 1835–1914*. London: RIBA.

McClintock, Anne. 1995. *Imperial Leather: Race, Gender, and Sexuality in the Colonial Conquest*. New York: Routledge.

Metcalf, Thomas. 1989. *An Imperial Vision: Indian Architecture and India's Raj*. Berkeley, CA: University of California Press.

Metcalf, Thomas. 1994. *Ideologies of the Raj*. Cambridge: Cambridge University Press.

Morris, Jan. 1986. *Stones of Empire: The Buildings of the Raj*, 2nd edn. Oxford: Oxford University Press.

O'Dwyer, Michael F. (ed.). 1889. *Monograph on Wood Manufactures in the Punjab: 1887–88*. Lahore: Civil and Military Gazette Press.

Pinney, Thomas (ed.). 1986. *Kipling's India: Uncollected Sketches, 1884–88*. London: Macmillan.

Poovey, Mary. 1995. *Making a Social Body: British Cultural Formation, 1830–1864*. Chicago, IL: University of Chicago Press.

Schmiechen, James. 1988. "The Victorians, the Historians, and the Idea of Modernism." *American Historical Review* 93(2): 287–316.

Serematakis, Nadia (ed.). 1994. *The Senses Still: Perception and Memory as Material Culture in Modernity*. Boulder, CO: Westview Press.

Sinha, Mrinalini. 1995. *Colonial Masculinity: The "Manly Englishman" and the "Effeminate Bengali" in the Late Nineteenth Century*. New York: Manchester University Press.

Stamp, Gavin. 1981. "British Architecture in India 1857–1947." *Journal of the Royal Society of Arts* 129: 129–33.

Steel, Flora Annie. 1888. *The Complete Indian Housekeeper and Cook*. London: Macmillan and Company.

Stoler, Ann Laura. 1995. *Race and the Education of Desire: Foucault's History of Sexuality and the Colonial Order of Things*. Durham, NC: Duke University Press.

Thompson, F. M. L. 1988. *The Rise of Respectable Society: A Social History of Victorian Britain, 1830–1900*. Cambridge, MA: Harvard University Press.

Tillotson, G. H. R. 1989. *The Tradition of Indian Architecture: Continuity, Controversy and Change Since 1850*. New Haven, CT: Yale University Press.

Upton, Dell. 1977. *Holy Things and Profane: Anglican Parish Churches in Colonial Virginia*. New Haven, CT: Yale University Press.

Upton, Dell. 1998. *Architecture in the United States*. Oxford: Oxford University Press.

Vidler, Anthony. 1992. *The Architectural Uncanny: Essays in the Modern Unhomely*. Cambridge, MA: The MIT Press.

White, Luise. 1990. *The Comforts of Home: Prostitution in Colonial Nairobi*. Chicago, IL: University of Chicago Press.

Wright, Gwendolyn. 1980. *Moralism and the Modern Home*. Chicago, IL: University of Chicago Press.

Unpublished Government Records

PPAP = Punjab Provincial Archives, Pakistan
  Home Department Proceedings: General, Medical and Sanitary
OIOC = Oriental and India Office Collections, London
  MSS European Manuscripts Collection

Published Government Records

Census of India, 1911. Vol. 14 (Punjab), Pt 1. Lahore: Civil and Military Gazette Press.

Journals and Newspapers

The Bungalow: A Paper for Anglo Indian Homes
The New York Times
The Punjab Magazine

HOME CULTURES   VOLUME 1, ISSUE 1.   REPRINTS AVAILABLE   PHOTOCOPYING   © BERG 2004
                  PP 83–88   DIRECTLY FROM THE   PERMITTED BY LICENSE PRINTED IN THE UK
                                          PUBLISHERS.   ONLY

BEN LANGLANDS AND NIKKI BELL

THE HOUSE OF OSAMA BIN LADEN

ARTISTS LANGLANDS AND BELL EXPLORE THE COMPLEX WEB OF RELATIONSHIPS LINKING PEOPLE AND ARCHITECTURE, AND THE CODED SYSTEMS OF CIRCULATION AND EXCHANGE WHICH SURROUND US. BASED IN LONDON, THEY HAVE BEEN COLLABORATING SINCE 1978 AND HAVE EXHIBITED THEIR WORK EXTENSIVELY INTERNATIONALLY INCLUDING THE SERPENTINE GALLERY, LONDON; MUSEUM OF MODERN ART, NEW YORK; VENICE BIENNALE; CENTRAL HOUSE OF THE ARTISTS, MOSCOW. EXAMPLES OF THEIR WORK CAN BE FOUND IN THE PERMANENT COLLECTIONS OF NUMEROUS MUSEUMS AND GALLERIES IN THE UK AND ABROAD.

In October 2002, Langlands and Bell spent two weeks traveling in Afghanistan researching the commission *The Aftermath of September 11 and the War in Afghanistan* for the Imperial War Museum, London.

Using a still and a digital video camera, Langlands and Bell recorded visits to numerous locations, including after a long and dangerous journey, the former home of Osama bin Laden at Daruntah, where he lived for a period in the late 1990s.

> Now used as a base by a local unit of the Hizb-I-Islami militia (Figure 1), bin Laden's home (Figure 2), situated on a promontory overlooking a lake in the mountains west of Jalalabad, is the subject of an interactive digital model, which allows virtual exploration of the house and its surroundings by means of a joystick. *The House of Osama bin Laden* is a collaboration with Tom Barker's V/SpaceLAB, which builds on principles established by Langlands and Bell and Tom Barker when they produced "The Artist's Studio" for the Turner Studio Residency at Petworth House in 2002.

The House of Osama bin Laden explores ways in which evidence of the identity or presence of a person may be discovered, revealed, or projected, in a locality after their departure. In the aftermath of September 11 Osama bin Laden could be seen to have attained a quasi-mythical status. At the time of making this work, the question remains: is he alive or is he dead? Where are his remains, or where is he hiding? Would we even recognize him if we saw him? While bearing testimony to his absence, the vacant house at Daruntah becomes through art a metaphor, for the elusive presence bin Laden maintains by the fact of his disappearance.

The house commands a panoramic view of its surroundings (Figure 3) and consists of several structures set in an area of rough ground littered with discarded spent and live munitions, abandoned military vehicles, and rusting hardware (Figure 4). The buildings comprise a modest three-roomed house (Figure 5) in the local vernacular with a small terrace and an external kitchen lean-to, a small mosque (Figure 6), and a bomb shelter/bunker (Figure 7). The latter two buildings were added by bin Laden specifically for his own use. The mosque is conventionally constructed out of local stone and concrete while the bunker is an unusual, partially excavated structure with walls made from stacked wooden ammunition boxes filled with rocks and earth. It is covered with an earth (Figure 8) and stone roof set on branches strengthened with ex-Soviet truck chassis.

Architecture is one of the most tangible records of the way we live. Buildings tend to encapsulate our hopes and fears at many levels while also reflecting the persistent human will to plan events. This is evident whether we are considering the monumental edifices of the twin towers in New York, or this modest group of structures at Daruntah. In both contexts we can discover a language of intentions in the character and fabric of the structure.

In the suspended realities offered by today's news media and entertainment industries, real experiences are often presented like a game, where life is an adventure, and war means excitement experienced from a safe vantage point. In *The House of Osama bin Laden* the instant reaction speeds, and phantasmagorical fun of the typical computer game have been neutralized. Langlands and Bell's non-spectacular approach emphasizes experience of place over the binary polarities of instant action versus instant outcome. In *The House of Osama bin Laden* you have no weapons as you explore the boundaries of a ghostly electronic world.

TECHNICAL OUTLINE AND PRODUCTION DETAILS

The House of Osama bin Laden is an interactive digital animation made by Langlands and Bell in collaboration with Tom Barker's V/SpaceLAB (see Virtual Reality Illustrations 1–3).

VR Ill. 1.

The production of the work was commissioned by the Imperial War Museum, London for the exhibition *Langlands & Bell—The House of Osama bin Laden* at the Imperial War Museum, London April 10–May 26, 2003.

The project was conceived and developed by Langlands and Bell from hundreds of photographs and measurements taken by the artists when they visited the house of Osama bin Laden at Daruntah in eastern Afghanistan in October 2002.

The artists collaborated with Tom Barker's V/SpaceLAB to produce an interactive digital model of Osama bin Laden's domain which allows "visitors" to interact and explore the house and its surroundings virtually by means of a joystick.

The House of Osama Bin Laden makes pioneering use of computer games technology to create a three-dimensional environment that allows visitors to walk freely around its digital world. The underlying technology of the work is based on a computer game called *Quake*, by ID software. Hundreds of images compiled by Langlands and Bell have been digitized and placed into a customized set of special effects libraries designed by Tom Barker called V/SpaceLAB. The V/SpaceLAB libraries facilitate transparency, translucency, lighting, and all the requirements to make a computer world convincing.

VR Ill. 2.

Images in V/SpaceLAB are treated as digital "wallpaper" textures and "wrapped" around the "3-dimensional objects" in the virtual model. The design mixes real and apparent 3D objects and surfaces. Finally the model is saved and processed, turning an ASCII text file into a computer binary file to be run by the *Quake* game engine. The binary file has additional information in it to describe shadow and sunlight.

The House of Osama bin Laden was on display at the

Imperial War Museum
London
April 10–May 26, 2003 and can be seen at

VR Ill. 3.

IMMA Irish Museum of Modern Art
Dublin
December 10, 2003–February 8, 2004

ACKNOWLEDGMENTS

Langlands and Bell would like to thank Tom Barker and Niki Holmes for their work on the production of the model, and Richard Wilding for additional digital artwork and design.

Figure 1
Members of the Hizb-i-Islami
militia currently based at the
house of Osama bin Laden,
Daruntah, Afghanistan.

Figure 3
View from the south room of
the house of Osama bin
Laden.

Figure 2
The house of Osama bin
Laden.

Figure 4
Machine gun post at the
entrance to the house of
Osama bin Laden.

Figure 5
Interior of the south room of
the house of Osama bin
Laden.

Figure 6
Mosque constructed by
Osama bin Laden at his
house in Daruntah,
Afghanistan.

Figure 7
Exterior of bunker constructed by Osama bin Laden behind his house at Daruntah, Afghanistan.

Figure 8
Detail of bunker wall made from ammunition boxes filled with stones, constructed by Osama bin Laden behind his house at Daruntah, Afghanistan.

HOME CULTURES

NOTES TO CONTRIBUTORS

- Articles should be approximately 5,000 to 8,000 words (but not exceeding 8,000 words in length unless by prior agreement please).
- They must include a three-sentence biography of the author(s) and an abstract.
- Interviews should not exceed 15 pages and do not require an author biography.
- Exhibition and book reviews are normally 500 to 1,000 words in length but review articles can be between 1,000 and 2,000 words.
- The Publishers will require a disk as well as a hard copy of any contributions.

From time to time, *Home Cultures* plans to produce special issues devoted to a single topic with a guest editor. Persons wishing to organize a topical issue are invited to submit a proposal which contains a 100-word description of the topic together with a list of potential contributors and paper subjects. Proposals are accepted only after a review by the Journal editors and in-house editorial staff at Berg Publishers.

MANUSCRIPTS

- Manuscripts should be submitted to:
  Clare Melhuish, Editorial Administrator, *Home Cultures*, Department of Anthropology, University College London, Gower Street, London WC1E 6BT or to <homecultures@ucl.ac.uk>.
- Manuscripts will be acknowledged and entered into the review process discussed below.
- Manuscripts without illustrations will not be returned unless the author provides a self-addressed stamped envelope.
- Submission of a manuscript to the journal will be taken to imply that it is not being considered elsewhere, in the same form, in any language, without the consent of the editor and publisher. It is a condition of acceptance by the editor of a manuscript for publication that the publishers automatically acquire the copyright of the published article throughout the world. *Home Cultures* does not pay authors for their manuscripts nor does it provide retyping, drawing, or mounting of illustrations.

STYLE

- US spelling and mechanicals are to be used. Authors are advised to consult The Chicago Manual of Style (14th Edition) as a guideline for style. Webster's Dictionary is our arbiter of spelling. We encourage the use of major subheadings and, where appropriate, second-level subheadings.
- Manuscripts submitted for consideration as an article must contain:
  – a title page with the full title of the article, the author(s) name and address
  – a three-sentence biography for each author.
- Do not place the author's name on any other page of the manuscript.

MANUSCRIPT PREPARATION

- Manuscripts must be typed double-spaced (including quotations, notes and references cited), on one side only, with at least one-inch margins on standard paper using a typeface no smaller than 12pts.
- The original manuscript and a copy of the text on disk (please ensure it is clearly marked with the word-processing program that has been used) must be submitted, along with original photographs (to be returned).
- Authors should retain a copy for their records.
- Any necessary artwork must be submitted with the manuscript.

FOOTNOTES

- Footnotes appear as 'Notes' at the end of articles.
- Authors are advised to include footnote material in the text whenever possible.
- Notes are to be numbered consecutively throughout the paper and are to be typed double-spaced at the end of the text
- *(Please do not use any footnoting or end-noting programs which your software may offer as this text becomes irretrievably lost at the typesetting stage.)*

REFERENCES

- The list of references should be limited to, and inclusive of, those publications actually cited in the text.
- References are to be cited in the body of the text in parentheses with author's last name, the year of original publication, and page number – e.g. (Rouch 1958: 45).
- Titles and publication information appear as 'References' at the end of the article and should be listed alphabetically by author and chronologically for each author.
- Names of journals and publications should appear in full. Film and video information appear as 'Filmography'.
- References cited should be typed double-spaced on a separate page.
- References not presented in the style required will be returned to the author for revision.

TABLES

- All tabular material should be part of a separately numbered series of 'Tables'.
- Each table must be typed on a separate sheet and identified by a short descriptive title.
- Footnotes for tables appear at the bottom of the table.
- Marginal notations on manuscripts should indicate approximately where tables are to appear.

FIGURES

All illustrative material: drawings, maps, diagrams, and photographs should be designated 'Figures'. They must be submitted in a form suitable for publication without redrawing.

- Drawings should be carefully done with India ink on either hard, white, smooth-surfaced board or good quality tracing paper. Ordinarily, computer-generated drawings are not of publishable quality.
- Color photographs are encouraged by the publishers. These will be reproduced in color in the print and on-line versions of the journal.
- Photographs should be glossy prints and should be numbered on the back to key with captions. Whenever possible, photographs should be 8 × 10 inches.
- The publisher also encourages artwork to be submitted as scanned files (300dpi or above ONLY) on disc or via email.
- All figures should be numbered consecutively.
- All captions should be typed double-spaced on a separate page.
- Marginal notations on manuscripts should indicate approximately where figures are to appear.
- While the editors and publishers will use all reasonable care in protecting all figures submitted, they cannot assume responsibility for their loss or damage. Authors are discouraged from submitting rare or non-replaceable materials. It is the author's responsibility to secure written copyright clearance on all photographs and drawings that are not in the public domain.

CRITERIA FOR EVALUATION

Home Cultures is a refereed journal. Manuscripts will be accepted only after review by both the editors and anonymous reviewers deemed competent to make professional judgments concerning the quality of the manuscript.

REPRINTS FOR AUTHORS

Twenty-five reprints of author's articles will be provided to the author free of charge. Additional reprints may be purchased upon request.

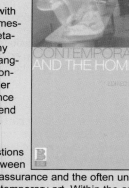